A Credible and Timely Word

Process Theology and Preaching

A Credible and Timely Word

Process Theology and Preaching

Clark M. Williamson
and
Ronald J. Allen

Chalice Press
St. Louis, Missouri

Library of Congress Cataloging–in–Publication Data

Williamson, Clark M.
    A credible and timely word : process theology and preaching / Clark
    M. Williamson and Ronald J. Allen.
1. Process theology.   2. Preaching   3. Sermons, American.
I. Allen, Ronald J. (Ronald James), 1949-
II. Title.
BT83.6.W55   1991   251   91-25311
ISBN 0-8272-0457-4

Contents

Bibliography

Chapter **1**

Introduction

This book attempts, in nontechnical ways, to bring together process theology and the responsibility of preaching the Christian faith. By "nontechnical," we intend to avoid a heavy-handed use of the specialized terms unique to process thought. We will, however, employ its major metaphors and categories. We write from the perspective of process theology, aware that this theology itself is "in process" and open-ended.

The major philosopher who has influenced process theology is Alfred North Whitehead. He described philosophical reflection as the "play of a free imagination, controlled by the requirements of coherence and logic."[1] The metaphor he used to "explain" philosophical thinking was that of an airplane flight: "It starts from the ground of particular observation; it makes a flight in the thin air of imaginative generalization; and it again lands for renewed observation rendered acute by rational interpretation."[2] Then the airplane takes off again for another flight through the thin air of imaginative generalization, on a never-ending journey toward understanding. Philosophical thinking ever remains "an experimental adventure"; its results are never final but both require and generate new interpretation.

What is true of process philosophy holds as well for process theology; its career has exemplified a capacity for self-correction and reinterpretation. Recently it has been reinterpreted by, and provided support for, theological efforts to deal with issues in black theology, feminist theology, and ecological theology.[3] Here we seek to bring process thought into conversation with practical theology as focused on the task of preaching.

One of our convictions is that preaching cannot begin to be adequate if it does not result from a sustained conversation between the biblical text and our deepest convictions about God. The only way to come within the understanding distance of the text is to read it convinced of what one nineteenth-century theologian called "God's complacent [unwarranted] affection for us."[4] One of the major problems with the doctrine of God propounded by traditional theism is that it not only cuts the ground out from under our conviction of God's affection for us but also works against those biblical texts that clearly assume or affirm that God interacts with God's creatures. Therefore we provide a chapter on models of God in which we correlate process ways of talking about God with the biblical witness and show that such ways of talking are appropriate to that witness. At the same time, we show how the variety of metaphorical ways of talking of God in process theology also are helpful in addressing some of the major critical issues of our time. Many of the metaphors for God that process theology develops are biblical; some are of more recent coinage. All would be disallowed by the tradition of classical theism with its emphasis on God's total immutability.

Process hermeneutics has shed much helpful light on how texts can be reinterpreted in ways appropriate not only to the Christian faith but to the human situation in our time. Among the many emphases of process hermeneutics, we lift up two for special consideration here. First, process hermeneutics stresses that a text *can* come to mean more than it has ever previously meant. The meaning of a text is not fixed, either in the text itself, in its pre-history, or in the subsequent history of its interpretation. Rather, when brought into conversation with the radically new questions of a post-Holocaust, ecocidal world (to name only two features characterizing the contemporary situation), interaction with the text can yield meanings never previously considered. Also, previously overlooked or ignored texts, such as all those from the Torah that articulate Israel's covenantal responsibilities toward the land (the earth, air, water, and living creatures), take on a new significance—a significance that Christians have largely denied by an allegorical, spiritualizing rendering of these texts, or have deliberately ignored. At the same time, we recognize that not every new interpretation is necessarily appropriate to the Christian faith, any more than it necessarily makes sense or is genuinely moral. Hence we also stress the importance of critically scrutinizing new meanings in the light of these three concerns.

Second, process hermeneutics takes a bifocal approach to texts. That is, the language of a text may be imprecise, fragmentary, or analogical, while on a deeper level the text may be at odds with a strict or literal reading of its language. Sometimes the "medium" of a text denies its "message," as when Matthew 7:1–5 interjects name-calling ("You hypocrite") into an otherwise beautiful teaching against being judgmental. What message does such a text communicate, when it does not practice the very thing it is preaching? The bifocal approach seeks to "read" each aspect of a text and arrive at a deeper possibility for understanding the Christian life. It tries to let the text's deeper insights criticize the distortions of that insight in the same text. Process hermeneutics attempts to move beyond the impasse in which the text itself often leaves us.

Also, because we think that the greatest evils of our time, the systemic ones, are seldom if ever addressed from the pulpit, we provide a chapter on sexism, racism, classism, the ecological crisis, and militarism—the five contemporary apocalyptic agents of destruction. We are convinced that preaching must increasingly learn how to address such issues in ways that help Christians understand the world in which they live, and live as Christians in the world they so understand. We are equally convinced that so-called "mainline" congregations today largely ignore the most burning issues facing us and thus fail to fulfill the central and age-old task of religion in any of its forms—namely, to help people figure out, in every new situation, who they are and what they ought to do. We think that an analysis of these five current systemic evils, with some process theological perspective on them, can help preachers increasingly carry out a now largely neglected part of their responsibility.

There is a crisis in the so-called "mainline" churches of America today, a crisis that goes deeper than the clearly apparent difficulties associated with diminishing numbers. This deeper crisis is theological in nature. Partly it has to do with the gap between much of the best theological thinking of the day and the teaching of the Christian faith that is heard from many pulpits.[5] We present this book as one attempt to start closing that gap.

It is not our point of view that all the problems with today's mainline churches stem from the failures of preachers and preaching and that none of them are due to theology and theologians. We readily admit that much contemporary theology is written in a jargon with which even other professional theologians have difficulty, and apparently by writers who give the impression that they would be offended were anyone actually to understand them. Still, we think that theologians and preachers have a lot to teach each other. Each of us teaches in a seminary and each of us, on occasion, preaches. Our experience is that theologizing and preaching can and should inform one another and that good theology will preach.

The assumption running throughout this book goes something like this: The purpose of preaching is to build up (edify, instruct) the church. Preaching cannot be limited to proclamation. To preach is also to teach the Christian faith. Preaching is teaching before it is anything else, and it is nothing else if it is not teaching the Christian faith. If preaching teaches the Christian faith, it can also, for example, evangelize: lead people to understand themselves in the light of the Christian faith. If, however, it fails to teach the Christian faith, what passes for evangelism will turn out to be teaching something other than, and less than, the Christian faith. Perhaps that something else will consist in offering to a yuppie audience the kinds of bromides that appeal to it, or in all the trite but not true appeals to culture-bound religion that people can bring to church. None of this, however, has anything to do with the gospel, the "evangel" in "evangelism."

To take another example, if preaching is teaching the Christian faith, it can also be prophetic articulation of the Christian witness in relation to the major social issues of the day. If it does not first (logically if not chronologically first) teach the Christian faith, however, its supposed prophetic witness will turn out to be little more than the advocacy of the preacher's favorite laundry list of social causes. While these causes may be fine ones, the congregation will not have been supplied with the links that connect them to the core witness of the Christian community. That is, the congregation will not have been given a chance to see how the stance taken on the social issue is appropriate to and required by the Christian faith. Church members deserve the opportunity to understand why people who take their Christian faith seriously should get behind this or that cause. Too often, mainline preachers present conclusions without arguments, leaving both themselves and their hearers buffaloed in the face of people who hold other, contrary positions and have arguments in support of them.

"Mainline" Protestants today are noticeably weak on evangelism (at least as far as the numbers are concerned) and comparatively strong on social witness (although, as a rule, more so in general assemblies and synods than in local congregations). We do not contend that learning how to be better teachers of the Christian faith will, by itself, "solve" the church's current lack of evangelical effectiveness or overcome immediately the leadership/followership gap that plagues mainline churches on social-ethical issues. At least, however, it will help preachers carry out one of the tasks to which they have been called and by which they have been claimed, and that is to be ministers of the word, teachers of the faith.

When preachers step into the pulpit, they face the most exhilarating and demanding of tasks, probably one at least as difficult as if not more difficult than that faced by members of other professions. Their task is to confront people with the gospel of Jesus Christ in such a way that again and again they are brought face to face with a *decision* as to whether they will understand themselves, in any ultimate sense, in terms of and only in terms of this gospel.

There are doubtless some who will take this stress on decision as characteristically existentialist and Bultmannian—and atypical, if not aberrant, for process theology. Process theology is ordinarily associated with themes of relationality and connectivity, while existentialism, with its stress on decision, is usually criticized (perhaps unfairly) for a view of persons as isolated individuals and for a view of faith as quarantined within individual subjectivity.

For process theology, however, it is precisely *because* we are interrelated with everything that goes into the making of us that we must *decide* how to constitute ourselves in relation to all that influences (flows into) us.[6] Decision, for Whitehead, makes up the very meaning of actuality; the "act" that an actual occasion commits is its decision as to how to constitute itself. In the terms coined by Catherine Keller, process theology affirms neither the "soluble" self nor the "separative" self.[7] The self that values relationships but cannot decide how to constitute itself is "soluble," dissolving into the relationships to which it is committed. The self that constitutes and asserts itself while suppressing the relationships that nurture and sustain it is "separative," confined within the narrow prison of its isolated ego. What is sought is persons who can value both themselves and their relations, persons who become the unique individuals they are both because of the way they decide to constitute themselves in the context of their relationships and because of the singular sets of relationships in which they participate. For process thought, the terms "individual" and "community" both represent abstractions. The concrete reality is the "individual-in-community," and the community in which we find ourselves is not limited to the human community. We human beings are constantly faced with the decision as to how to understand ourselves, a point on which process thought is no less insistent than existentialism.[8]

Hence we claim that one of the chief functions of preaching is to confront people, again and again, with the question of how they will decide to understand, and hence constitute, themselves. And that question is whether in any ultimate sense they will understand themselves (or whether "we" will, since the question is addressed to preachers as well) only in terms of the love of God graciously offered to each and all, and in terms of the dual command of God that we love God *with* all our selves and our neighbors *as* ourselves. That is to say, the gospel is not a circle with one center but an ellipse with two foci.[9] The one focus is the love of God graciously (freely) offered to each and all. The other is the command of God that we love God and one another even as we have been loved by God.

The elliptical character of the gospel is what some process thinkers call its "dipolar" reality: The gospel has two poles, neither of which may be ignored without seriously misunderstanding it as a result. If we take the love of God freely offered to us as the *only point* of the gospel, conveniently forgetting the command of God that justice be done to each and all, we will plunge headlong into what Dietrich Bonhoeffer called "cheap grace," which he defined as "forgiveness of sins proclaimed as a general truth, the love of God taught as the Christian 'conception' of God...the justification of sin without the justification of the sinner."[10] Knowing the truth of the gospel is a transformative knowing; cheap grace is non-transformative. On the other hand, if we take the command of God to do justice to all those whom God loves as the *only point,* while forgetting the empowering and redeeming grace of God, we fall just as quickly into works-righteousness.

If we forget the gospel altogether, our preaching will likely fall into one or the other of the two main ecclesiastical ruts of the day: crisis intervention or institutional maintenance. Crises are important (particularly to those going through them) and institutions need to be maintained, but the question of why *this* institution needs to be maintained should be asked, and many of the crises pastors have to deal with could be avoided in the first place. That is, many personal crises occur because of intellectual and moral confusion: People do not know how to *understand* themselves and the world in which they live in relation to ultimate reality, nor consequently *how to live* morally in a world so understood. Preachers as teachers of the Christian faith could use the sermon to help people come to understand who they are and how they should live in the light of the gospel.

Every time one of us seeks to teach the Christian faith, we need to ask ourselves three questions. If we begin, as we usually do, with a scriptural text as an earlier piece of Christian witness and seek to understand (interpret) it in order to re-present its witness to the contemporary church, we need to pose three questions to that text—or, more properly, to our interpretation of it (there are no uninterpreted texts).

First, if I understand this text correctly, is its witness appropriate to the gospel of Jesus Christ? Is it a proper Christian witness? We may learn new things about the gospel from a given text, but we may also learn that any text is infected with elements quite contrary to the gospel.

Here we need to remember that process theology's approach to texts is not limited to hermeneutics. Some texts, or some aspects of any text, may simply need to be rejected. The de-ideologizing power of the love who is God simply requires, for example, that after Auschwitz we grant no authority to anti-Judaism in any biblical text. The same holds true for sexism and racism. In other words, we need to wrestle with the text in the light of our deepest understanding of the gospel, in order that our grasp of the gospel may be deepened and in order that we do not proclaim as central to the Christian faith what was merely incidental to the text. We need, in other words, to grasp the deeper insight, the heart of the matter, and at least sometimes to oppose those aspects of the text that themselves oppose the gospel.

Second, we need to ask of the text's witness another question: What sense does this make? How is it true or how does it work? Without pretending that how we understand things ought to be the norm for everybody, and without denying that different peoples and cultures understand things differently, we can nonetheless say this: If the preacher does not understand the point, neither will the congregation. The reason this question is important is that the gospel of Jesus Christ is a truth-claim; it claims to be true, not just a passing fancy. If it does not claim to be true, it makes no claim upon us to take it seriously. The claim it makes is that the only authentic way in which we as human beings can understand ourselves in any ultimate sense and live accordingly is in terms of God's love graciously offered even to us and God's love of the neighbor on whose behalf God demands justice. A God who makes no claims or demands should not be taken seriously; indeed, such a God is not even interesting. Any other way in which we might ultimately understand ourselves is misleading. The ultimate truth about you and me is not our nationality, not our skin color, not our gender, not our income level; to understand ourselves ultimately in such terms is idolatrous and destructive. Such indeed is precisely the heart of the complaint of black and feminist theologians against racism and sexism, that the destructiveness of racism and sexism result from taking sex and race as absolute and ultimate whereas they are relative and finite. Ultimately there is only one truth about us: that the only reason we count or matter is because we matter to the One who is ultimate, the One who loves us in spite of knowing us perfectly, and the only proper response to knowing that God loves us is to love the neighbor in God in return.[11] We say "love the neighbor in God" because process theology imagines God panentheistically (*pan* = all, *en* = in, *theos* = God: everything is in God). In God is precisely where the neighbor is and that is the ultimate, meta-ethical reason why we should love the neighbor. In classic theological terms, the transformative knowledge of God's love freely offered to us is justification—our awareness that we are loved, affirmed and accepted by God as the only final ground of our worth. And the new and transformed life lived in love and service to the neighbor, which is the claim God lays upon us, is sanctification.

Third, we need to ask of any text (or of our understanding of it) whether its message is morally plausible. Because the gospel also commands that justice be done, moral concerns are part and parcel of any preaching that would be appropriate to the gospel as they are to the understanding of God as the One who loves all others. Yet we know that some passages of scripture have long been subject to interpretation in plainly unjust ways. Some have been used to justify slavery, others to rationalize the suppression of women, others to warrant the denigration of Jews, some to support oppressive governments, and yet others to excuse despoiling the environment. Nor are we unaware that the injustice was never merely verbal, although the first injustice is usually against language. So if a text seems unjust in these or other ways, we must seek the deeper meaning in it or its context in the light of which to preach against the injustice. For example, no biblical book contains more hideous defamations of Jews than does John's gospel (see especially chapter 8). Nor does any biblical book contain a more beautiful description of what the Christian life is and ought to be (John 13:34). Surely it is possible to criticize John's uglier moments in the light of his own deeper insight.

We want to call attention to another book on process theology and preaching and to the relationship between that book and this one. Six process theologians and biblical scholars (William A. Beardslee, John B. Cobb, Jr., David J. Lull, Russell Pregeant, Theodore J. Weeden, Sr., and Barry A. Woodbridge) have recently published *Biblical Preaching on the Death of Jesus*.[12] A full review of this text will not be attempted here. Instead, we want to lift up its distinctive contribution and show how these two books have a complementary relation to each other.

The authors of *Biblical Preaching on the Death of Jesus* work with the insights of process hermeneutics (which will be discussed more fully below in a chapter by that title), the aim of which "is to hold contrasting insights in tension so that each may be creatively transformed."[13] Such a mode of interpretation employs the disparities between the biblical world and our own so as "to open new horizons" among contemporary listeners. This "expanding of the hearers' world" places Christian preaching in the service of Christian freedom, understood as the freedom "to be more related, both to the Spirit and to one another; freedom from the compulsiveness of the past; and freedom to enter more fully and spontaneously into the life of faith and love."[14] Normatively, preaching "should serve directly in the liberation of the hearer."[15] Among the chief emphases of the authors is the concern that such preaching free contemporary Christians from both an uncritical (if unconscious) rejection of the biblical world and an equally uncritical acceptance of the modern world, both of which inhibit their ability to hear the gospel.

Christian preaching serves Christian freedom in this way, and as the insight involved here is unpacked in the book, the full range of freedom/liberation issues is addressed. We are called forward by the claim of God's justice and love to become God's covenant partners in the effort to overcome injustice and torment in the world. The focus of the book is on the "proposals" or "suggestions," sometimes conflicting, found in texts or in the strained relationship between biblical texts and the contemporary world.

The authors understand such proposals on the order of Whitehead's theory of propositions,[16] a theory that will be important in our chapter on process hermeneutics. Whitehead understood a proposition as a fusion of an actuality and a novel possibility. Every proposition is true or false, but the important function of false propositions is that they pave the way for the advance into novelty. "Error is the price which we pay for progress."[17] A proposition invites a creative, imaginative response, "calls it forth," and the possibility always exists that a false but interesting proposition might be seriously entertained and made true. That the congregation of which I am a member takes seriously its Christian responsibility for the homeless and destitute and performs exemplary Christian service on their behalf is a false, but interesting, proposition. It would be even more interesting were it true.

Using such key insights, Cobb, Beardslee, *et al.*, articulate an understanding of preaching as making proposals to the congregation, proposals that invite them to move out of oppositional ways of *and the greatest of these is a CLEAR SENTENCE!*

thinking and feeling, that they might be open to the ways in which God seeks creatively to transform us from the narrowness, sinfulness, and limitations of our past. The preacher's primary task is "to remove obstacles so that the congregation may hear what the Spirit is trying to say to each member."[18]

Neither is the relationship between *Biblical Preaching and the Death of Jesus* and this book oppositional. It is complementary, with enough differences to make the two an interesting contrast: In process thought, contrast is the opposite of incompatibility. Many of the differences, we suspect, are matters of emphasis. Our approach is more appreciative of the existential dimension within process thought itself than is theirs, with the result that we do see preaching somewhat more in the Reformation tradition of confronting the congregation with the gospel than in the style of presenting proposals to it. Partly this is the result of our awareness, based on another work we have written, of the reluctance of mainline churches to ask what the church has to say that no one else has to say.[19] Also, we are keenly interested in restoring to the clergy a sense of their responsibility to be teachers of the Christian faith, which we see as one of the keys to the reinvigoration of the so-called "mainline" churches. These churches, now often referred to as "old line" or "side line," have too often become the "What's my line?" churches (the reader will excuse the hyperbole). Hence our insistence on the gospel as the norm of appropriateness and ground of the authority of Christian teaching plays a pronounced role in our approach to Christian preaching.

One way to characterize the differences between these two books, with some overstatement, would be to say that theirs concentrates on *how* Christian faith is taught, while we concentrate more on *what* is taught. At the same time, our sense of things is that it is also the case that in most mainline congregations there is virtually no Christian preaching/teaching going on with respect to the major moral/ethical dilemmas and crises that confront the world today. Several careful sociological studies of preaching confirm this sense. One has a chapter on "Ministers as Moral Guides," which it entitles: "The Silent Majority."[20] Hence we sketch out the major systemic evils of our time and indicate some of the resources provided by process thought for addressing them. We hope to encourage and give moral support to clergy to help their congregations understand who they are as Christians and what they ought to do in relation to these systemic injustices.

Our concerns are hardly absent from *Biblical Preaching on the Death of Jesus*, any more than its concerns are absent from this text. But, as is inevitably the case in theology, where none of us ever seems to get wholly free from context and biography, differences of emphasis and concern contribute spice to the conversation.

So we have written this book on the relation between process theology and preaching. Clark Williamson initially drafted the chapters on models of God, systemic injustice, and process hermeneutics. Ron Allen did the primary work on the interpretation of biblical texts. Each of us contributed a sermon to the chapter of sermons at the end. All chapters were rewritten after being read by the other author. We want to thank three people especially for their help with this project: William A. Beardslee, for reading an earlier version of the manuscript, and Charles Blaisdell and David Polk, for reading a later version of it.

We dedicate the book to our colleagues at Christian Theological Seminary who are toiling in the vineyard of theological education while we are both, happily, on research leave. It's the least we could do for them.

Notes

[1]Alfred North Whitehead, *Process and Reality*, Corrected Edition (New York: The Free Press, 1978), p. 5.

[2]*Ibid.*

[3]See, e.g., Henry James Young, *Hope in Process: A Theology of Social Pluralism* (Philadelphia: Fortress Press, 1990), Charles Birch and John B. Cobb, *The Liberation of Life: From the Cell to the Community* (Cambridge: Cambridge University Press, 1981), and Rita Brock, *Journeys by Heart* (New York: Crossroad, 1988).

[4]Alexander Campbell, *The Christian System*, Reprint Edition (Salem, NH: Ayer Company, 1988), p. 17.

[5]We have recently published a book on the need of clergy, particularly those in the "mainline" churches, to rediscover and reinvigorate the teaching function of the ministry. See *The Teaching Minister* (Louisville: Westminster/ John Knox Press, 1991).

[6]"Influence" is often used as "influence upon" another. We use it here in the sense of its Latin roots (*in* + *fluere* = to flow in) as connoting internal, not

merely external, relations to the world. In the technical language of process philosophy, the category of freedom and determination holds that we are not reducible to our relationships, that there is always "a remainder for the decision of the subject-superject of that concrescence." See Whitehead, *Process and Reality*, p. 27f. As he puts it, "'decision' cannot be construed as a casual adjunct of an actual entity. It constitutes the very meaning of actuality" (*Ibid.*, p. 43). Langdon Gilkey finds this to be a strong existential expression in contemporary ontology: *Naming the Whirlwind* (Indianapolis: Bobbs-Merrill, 1969), p. 366, n. 1.

[7]See her *From A Broken Web* (Boston: Beacon Press, 1986).

[8]Indeed, it is often taken as a hallmark of all "modern" thought since Kant that what it means to be an authentic human being is to take responsibility for oneself, particularly for one's self-actualization and self-creation. What distinguishes process thought on this topic is its understanding of the process/ relational nature of the self, not the lack of stress on decision.

[9]The metaphor for the gospel as an ellipse with two foci was coined by Albrecht Ritschl, *The Christian Doctrine of Justification and Reconciliation*, tr. H. R. Mackintosh (New York: Charles Scribner's Sons, 1900). The two foci are those in Ritschl's title: "justification" by God's free grace, "reconciliation" (the kingdom of God, justice) as God's purpose.

[10]Dietrich Bonhoeffer, *The Cost of Discipleship*, tr. R. H. Fuller (New York: Macmillan, 1963), p. 45f.

[11]Charles Hartshorne has magisterially developed the dual understanding of God according to which God is the One, and the only One, who perfectly knows (sympathizes with) all others, and of our love for God as entailing sympathy with all those with whom God is sympathetic. See his *Beyond Humanism* (Chicago: Willett, Clark & Co., 1937), p. 54f.

[12]William A. Beardslee, John B. Cobb, Jr., David J. Lull, Russell Pregeant, Theodore J. Weeden, Sr., and Barry A. Woodbridge, *Biblical Preaching on the Death of Jesus* (Nashville: Abingdon Press, 1989).

[13]*Ibid.*, p. 9.

[14]*Ibid.*, p. 30f.

[15]*Ibid.*, p. 32.

[16]*Ibid.*, p. 35.

[17]Whitehead, *Process and Reality*, p. 187.

[18]Beardslee, Cobb, *et al.*, *Biblical Preaching on the Death of Jesus*, p. 37.

[19]*The Teaching Minister* (Louisville: Westminster/John Knox Press, 1991).

[20]See, e.g., Rodney Stark, *et al.*, *Wayward Shepherds: Prejudice and the Protestant Clergy* (New York: Harper & Row, 1971), chap. 5.

Chapter 2

Models of God

Theologians have always recognized that there is something pretentious, if not idolatrous, in thinking about God. Yet theologians, like the church itself, have never been able to maintain an absolute silence about God, because God is at the center of the Christian proclamation of Jesus Christ. Indeed, everything Christians want to say is somehow about God and God's grace, or else it might as well not be said. What makes a statement a Christian statement or a theological statement is that it expresses our concern with ultimate reality as graciously disclosed to us in Jesus Christ.

One way Christians have taken out of this impasse between the inability to talk about God and the unwillingness not to praise our redeemer is to assert that all our statements about God are negative. That is, the so-called "negative theology" contends that when we speak of God we do not so much say what God is as what God is not. So we say that God is "infinite," not in order to specify anything about God but to deny that God is finite, "in-finite" being a purely negative concept. Yet surely this is too high a price to pay if our language about God is to be appropriate to the gospel of God's love graciously offered to each and all and God's command that justice

15

be done to each and all. When we say, for example, that "God is love" (1 John 4:8), we certainly intend to say more than God is not malicious, perhaps only "indifferent" or "immutable" (also negative terms).

The strength of negative theology lies in its contention that all our models and metaphors are inadequate to give voice to the mystery of God. In this it is surely right; all our knowledge of God is a "learned ignorance." For that matter, no idea of another human being even begins to express the concrete reality of that person or serves as anything more than a pitiably inadequate pointer to her. Yet some ways of talking about another human being will be comparatively more adequate than others. Such words as "aloof, detached, harsh" do not adequately describe the person who is actually "kind, patient, gentle." So it is with God as God is witnessed to in the Christian faith: Some models of—or metaphors for—God are more appropriate and adequate than others.

The way taken here out of the impasse posed by the difficulty in talking about God will be to say that although all our forms and symbols for God are "fallible,"[1] some are more fallible than others. And while we may talk about God or, more precisely, about the models and metaphors that we use to point to God, we may not do so absentmindedly, forgetful of the fact that it is fallible human beings who are doing the talking. Some of our models for God are more appropriate to the norms of the Christian faith than are others, more intelligible in the light of our experience than others, and more helpful in face of the challenges we face in the ecological-nuclear age in which we live.

In this chapter we will highlight two important models of God, the first drawn from the Christian tradition, the second a more recent one inspired by such writers as Charles Hartshorne and Alfred North Whitehead. We will suggest that the limitations or contradictions of the traditional model of God render it less appropriate to the Christian faith, less intelligible, and less helpful than the alternative. We will submit that the alternative process-relational model of God is more appropriate, credible, and helpful. And we will focus on some of the metaphors for God and the relation between God and the world that have been developed in the tradition of process reflection upon God. It is more helpful to engage in a conversation with scripture, and in addressing the task of preaching, with these metaphors in mind than with the more traditional model of God.

The Traditional Model

Most Christians, including most Christian preachers, have probably not given a lot of time to thinking critically about the model or models of God with which they operate. There are understandable reasons why this might be so. Nonetheless, the likely result is that many of us have a kind of workaday theology (in the sense of a doctrine of God) that is more like a smorgasbord approach to eating—a little bit of this and that, each bit seemingly attractive—than like a considered approach to good nutrition. Experience with theological students indicates that this is so— specifically, that these students, later to be preachers, hold a "formal" doctrine of God that they can express but which is of little use to them in times of crisis, when they long for other kinds of things to say about God but do not know what those other things would be. Yet they often do not call into question and rethink their formal or more traditional view. Here we propose to do exactly that.

The classical doctrine of God as developed in the church of the first several centuries tended toward understanding God along the lines "of the transcendent absolute of much speculative philosophy: necessary, impersonal, unrelated, independent (*a se*), changeless, eternal."[2] Not only so, but God was also considered not merely as necessary, impersonal, unrelated, etc., but as *in all respects* (not merely in some) unrelated, eternal, changeless, independent, and incapable of being affected or moved by the fate of God's creatures. Obviously, it is one thing to say that God's being and God's divine character are necessary, that God cannot fail to be—and, specifically, to be *God*. It is quite another matter to say that God's experience or knowledge of the contingent and accidental affairs of the world is necessary, and that, therefore, God must always have foreknown the future in all its details. How God could "necessarily" know the non-necessary, the accidental and contingent, has never been satisfactorily explained. Yet the tradition affirmed God's necessity in all respects, not just in some. Nor is it at all clear how the eternal absolute of speculative philosophy is an appropriate

thank you Mr. Poopsandut

model for bringing to expression the covenantally related, engaged God of the biblical witness.

In other words, although the Christian and Jewish traditions clearly wanted to affirm that God is related to us, genuinely personal, responsive to creaturely needs, and involved in history and acting in it, nonetheless the model of God that emerged in the life of the church stressed that God is absolutely noncontingent, "changeless in the sense of participating in and relating to no change, purely spiritual instead of in any fashion material, unaffected and thus seemingly unrelated and even unrelatable to the world."[3] Were such a God to relate to the world, "he" (the pronoun here seems apt) could do so only by intervening in it, supernaturally. Also, if necessity, changelessness, and the lack of becoming and relationality are our very definition of what it is to be supremely real, then it is no wonder that along with this went a progressive loss of the sense of the "reality, value, or meaning of the changing, temporal, material world, and of earthly human and historical life in time."[4] Whether such a view of God is appropriate to the gospel of God's unbounded love, and whether it is intelligible, are two necessary questions.

Yet in our time it is equally important to ask what help such a view of God can be to us when the very continuing existence of the material world and of human life is up for grabs. What would the traditional view have to say to us except, perhaps, that whatever happens to the world could not possibly make any difference to God, God being immutable, and therefore is not finally important?

The conviction that we cannot know God because God is "both invisible and ineffable" began to gain ground early in the history of the church.[5] Clement of Alexandria quotes as his authorities on this point such writers as Plato, Orpheus, Solon, and Empedocles, and interprets the biblical witness to God in the light of their views. He argues from this premise that God is "infinite not in the sense of measureless extension but in the sense of being without dimensions or boundaries, and therefore without shape or name."[6] All that our names for God can do is to "point to the power of the Almighty."[7] Clement fails to note that the terms "power" and "almighty" ought, also, in his perspective, to be no more than pointers to the mystery of God. He plays favorites among his names, and, without justifying it, takes "power" to be what is really divine about God, that to which other terms point.

As Clement's example shows, traditional theism not only suffers from internal strains but from an uneasy relation to the biblical witness in which God is said quite directly to disclose God's name to Moses (Exodus 3). Another instance in which we see this uneasy relation is in Origen's concern to answer the question of how God can be said by scripture to repent or undergo a change of mind when we already know, apart from scripture, that God does not do these things.[8] Although scripture refers to God's repenting on several occasions, Origen's commitment to God's foreknowledge of the future means that this cannot be, God cannot repent. The deeper issue for Origen, of course, is that God cannot change at all, in any respect. Origen's way out of his dilemma, that scripture refers to God as doing precisely what Origen "already knows" God cannot possibly do, is to distinguish God "as he is in himself" from God as involved with human affairs. In "himself," God does not change; but in order to keep us from thinking that we are not free God "acts as if he did not know the future in your case."[9] Yet God does know the future, for Origen; how then are we free? Must God deceive us in order to convince us to be responsibly free?

Consistently with this view, Augustine argues that God is "untouched by want or change, nowhere does he look for any good which may increase him, nowhere does he fear any evil that may diminish him."[10] We human beings, members as we are of one another as well as of the whole web of life, are diminished by what diminishes others and enhanced by what enhances others, but according to Augustine this is not so for God because God is "immutable being," incapable of being affected by what happens to others.[11]

In the eleventh century Anselm summed up the traditional view of God:

But it is obvious that whatever good thing the supreme nature is, it is in the highest degree. It is, therefore, supreme being, supreme justness, supreme wisdom, supreme truth, supreme goodness, supreme greatness, supreme beauty, supreme immortality, supreme incorruptibility, supreme immutability, supreme blessedness, supreme eternity, supreme power, supreme unity; which is nothing else than supremely being, supremely living, etc.[12]

Anselm's view of God as "supreme immutability" was purchased at a high price. We note this in his prayerful question to God: "How art thou compassionate, and, at the same time, passionless?" Noting that if God is passionless God cannot feel sympathy, Anselm wonders "whence cometh so great consolation to the wretched?" His answer is reminiscent of Origen's explanation of God's repentance: "Thou art compassionate in terms of our experience, and not compassionate in terms of thy being." While "we experience the effects of compassion...thou dost not experience the feeling."[13] In other words, God merely seems to be compassionate toward us, but does not actually experience compassion for us because to do so would be to be mutable. Little wonder, therefore, that critics like Gilkey remark that, on this view, not only is God unrelated and unrelatable to the world but that, to boot, the value, meaning, and reality of the world and all that is in it is downplayed.

Shortcomings of the Classical Model

Although some of them have been mentioned, the deficiencies of classical theism need to be summarized. As a supernatural, interventionist model, it interprets faith as belief in the occurrence of certain ostensibly supernatural events. Faith thereby becomes "an arbitrary affair unless adequate reasons for belief can be given—a prospect that appears extremely unlikely."[14] It makes of God the one who can intervene (perhaps in the last act) and save us from our foolishness. At the same time it creates the problem of why God has not already done so. Where was God during the Holocaust, for example, and did God not hear the prayers of the slaves for freedom during the first few hundred years of American history? Also, by placing such responsibility on God for solving our problems, the traditional model deprives human beings of the freedom to act responsibly.

If God in God's all-powerfulness determines everything, if nothing takes place without God's deliberation,[15] how are our actions our own? How are they significant to God? How can we be free? The idea of God as all-powerful, immutable in all respects, and knowing the future in detail simply cannot be reconciled with the reality of human freedom and responsibility. Nor can things human or things earthly be of any ultimate importance to a God to whom nothing can be added, to a God incapable of experience and change. If we, our lives and our actions, along with the rest of the created order, make no difference to God, then the ultimate and final truth is that what happens on and to the earth, what we do and fail to do, are simply and finally unimportant. Our lives matter finally if and only if they matter to the One who is final; if we do not matter to God, the final truth is that we do not matter. Above all, in this nuclear-ecological age, we need a model of God that will enable us to understand both how we are empowered to act freely and responsibly and how and why our doing so matters to God.

So far, we have offered two criticisms of the traditional model of God: that it is incoherent and that it is ethically deficient, i.e., it fails to provide a reason why, in the final analysis, we should be moral. We would be remiss if we failed to point out that the classical model is inappropriate to the Christian faith. Long ago Alfred North Whitehead pointed out that when it came to thinking about God, the Christian tradition largely ignored the central disclosure of God at its heart. It continued to think of God in terms and metaphors that were prevalent prior to its "Galilean origin," and so fashioned God in the image of an imperial ruler, or of a ruthless moral energy, or of an abstract philosophical principle (Aristotle's "unmoved mover"). "The brief Galilean vision of humility" disclosed to us in Jesus Christ was allowed to flicker "throughout the ages, uncertainly."[16] In tentatively developing his own doctrine of God, Whitehead returned to what the church largely ignored—"the Galilean origin of Christianity"—and its alternative suggestion, which emphasized neither the ruling Caesar, nor the ruthless moralist, nor the unmoved mover. Instead, said Whitehead, "it dwells upon the tender elements in the world, which slowly and in quietness operate by love."[17] We saw above how Clement of Alexandria, in developing his doctrine of God, turned first to Plato, Empedocles, Orpheus, and Solon, and then interpreted the biblical witness in terms of the constraints established by their thought. Neither Clement nor the entire classical tradition bothered to argue the appropriateness of their view of God's utter immutability either biblically or theologically.

An Alternative Model

Ancient Greek thought, which so heavily influenced the early church, took objects of ordinary perception as its paradigmatic cases of reality. In this way, an object such as a gray stone came to exemplify the two basic categories of interpretation of classical thought. "Gray" was understood as an attribute or property of the underlying reality of the stone, which in turn was conceived in terms of "substance" or "being." Hence, reality was understood in terms of unrelated substances undergoing only external and accidental adventures of change as indicated by alterations in their attributes. So God could be conceived as a substance or being of whom we could know only the attributes.

The process-relational model of God begins with a different starting point, taking our awareness of our own existence as experiencing subjects as the basis of our fundamental concepts.[18] Totally unlike the notion of substances, which are nontemporal and nonrelated, the "very being of the self is relational or social; and it is nothing if not a process of change involving the distinct modes of present, past, and future."[19] Always embodied (there are no disembodied selves), by means of the body the self both is affected by and affects, interacts with, a much larger whole of reality. Because it is affected by others who change and differ, the self is as temporal as it is social.

If we develop a model of God from this basic awareness of the self, then God would be genuinely social and temporal, affected by others as well as affecting them, and utterly "different from the wholly timeless and unrelated Absolute of traditional theism."[20] The categorically unique status of God—God's perfection, or what it is that makes God God—would now be understood in terms of God's being "the self-surpassing surpasser of all."[21] God's perfection is no longer thought of as completely static and asocial, but as the unique or perfect instance of creative becoming and relationality. To put it in slightly different terms, the difference between God and any other subject is that God acts upon and is acted upon by *all* others, whereas each of us interacts only with *some* others. Or to take yet another tack, whereas the human self is incarnate in the world, it is so in a highly circumscribed way interacting with a limited and external environment. God's "body is the whole universe of nondivine beings," with each of which God's relation is immediate and direct.[22]

What God Does

Any model of God must tell us what God does and do so in ways that are appropriate to the gospel, credible, and morally plausible.

A chief liability of traditional theism arises precisely at this point. Its view of God as occasionally intervening in the course of worldly affairs, especially when brought into contact with the reality of evil, fails at every point. A God who could have prevented or stopped slavery but did not hardly expresses in such a failure to act the love of God for each and all or the command of God that justice be done to each and all. Nor is this view credible. We cannot conceive of an omnipresent God who could not intervene. Morally, the view that God will, nevertheless, take care of things, relieves us of the moral responsibility to do so on the grounds that God, some day, will.

On the alternative model developed in process theology, God does several things. First, God creates everything that is. Because process thought thinks of actuality as composed of events of becoming, events that are social and temporal, it points out that without God there would be nothing. What process theology means by the doctrine of "creation out of nothing" (*creatio ex nihilo*) is not that there ever was a time when there was God and nothing else, but that without God there would be nothing else. The traditional view that there was a "time" before time began when God existed in isolated grandeur surrounded by "nothing" is a literalized myth which, in this form, process theology rejects.

When Whitehead began to write about God, he did so because he had concluded that the final metaphysical analysis left us with the same problem faced by Plato. The problem was (or is) that if the world finally is analyzable into two realities, the ongoing flux of creativity on the one hand, and a realm of potentiality or possibility on the other, how are they ever gotten together? Unless there is some agent, said Whitehead, who can grade the possibilities into relevance for the ongoing flux of creativity, nothing actual will ever happen. Whitehead understood each new event as having to take into account a new past actual world, on which it needed a new perspective. But this new perspective, by definition, could not come from the past. Nor could the new occasion generate it, because the question of how that occasion would itself arise had first to be answered. Hence, Whitehead first introduced God into his metaphysical reflection, referring to God as the "principle of concretion," i.e., the principle by means of which concrete actuality emerged.[23] Later, in *Process and Reality*, this "picture" would change and God would become an actuality, an agent, in whose envisagement the possibilities are housed.[24] One reason why it is important to note that for process theology there would be nothing without God, is that we want to avoid giving the impression that the socially related God of process thought is seriously subject to an independent universe. God is affected by all others, in process theology, and perfectly so, but God is affected by nothing that God has not previously effected.

Second, when God's creative activity is understood as offering the novel aim at becoming around which events not only are enabled to arise but to take into themselves the richness of accumulated value that is the past, God is also seen to be the ground of our relation to all that has gone on before. The depth of experience—its thickness, the rich ways in which the past is present with us in contemporary experience as a great cloud of witnesses—is because of God's doing. Were we forced to live only on the plane of the present, knowing only immediate experience and novelty, not only would we be unable to recognize novelty when we saw it but we would be condemned to shallow, one-dimensional lives. The more of the past we are able to appreciate, the richer our present experience, the greater the range of our future possibilities, and the more significant our freedom.

Third, God not only creates us, but creates us as free, partially self-creating creatures. We human beings not only experience ourselves as free but, in a deeper sense, realize that freedom is unavoidable. That is, to be a human being is to decide how to understand oneself and how to constitute oneself. If no possibilities were open to us other than what the automatic consequences of the past allowed and necessitated, we would be nothing more than cogs in a cosmic mechanism. But this is in direct contradiction to our experience of ourselves as free to constitute ourselves, albeit always in relation to a context. Because God offers to us in each moment the highest relevant possibility for our becoming, "it is by virtue of the presence of God that I experience a call to be more than I have been and more than my circumstances necessitate that I be"; in other words, "it is by God's grace that I am free."[25]

So far we have said three things: God is the ground of our being and becoming, without whom neither we nor anything else would be at all; God is the ground of our relation to the past; God is the ground of our freedom. One more thing must be said about what

God does. Because God is genuinely and not just apparently social, God not only *acts upon* but *interacts with* all others. Not only is God unsurpassably active in the sense of "doing all that could conceivably be done by any one individual for all others," but God is "unsurpassably passive, being open to all that could be conceivably done or suffered by anyone as something that is also done to God."[26] We may trust God unqualifiedly because God is always doing everything for us that it is possible and appropriate for God to do. God may not always do for us everything that we want God to do, but that is another matter. It is only appropriate to ask God to do for us those things that only God can do; the rest is up to us. We may be unqualifiedly loyal to God because God, by accepting us and all others into God's everlasting life, redeems our lives from transience and insignificance. How we decide to understand and constitute ourselves, who we are and what we do, matters because it matters to God. Our faith in the meaningfulness and worthwhileness of who we are and what we do is the faith that is justified by God's gracious acceptance of us. God is Redeemer as well as Creator, Omega as well as Alpha.

In these functions of God we see the relation between faith and justice. First, God regards each and all of God's creatures as of intrinsic value, and desires that each one actualize its highest possibilities. Second, God desires that each enjoy the greatest possible richness of experience. Third, God intends that each one be free and self-determining. Fourth, God promises that each one is loved, everlastingly taken into the divine life, saved, redeemed. Because God unfailingly undergoes whatever happens to each of the creatures, what we do or fail to do to others we do or fail to do to God. Faith demands justice because God demands justice. "There is just one sphere of action, this-world-in-God."[27] God redeems us from insignificance and, by promising that we are justified by grace through faith, offers us the freedom to love our neighbors as ourselves, to cease being closed in upon ourselves. God does everything for each and all of us that God can possibly do, leaving it up to us to do all those things that only we can do if they are to be done at all.

Old Metaphors for God

The classical model of God as all-powerful and unmovable, seeing each detail of the future in one *totum simul*, was expressed in a dominant metaphor, that of a king ruling over his kingdom. The classical model was not only hierarchical but monarchical and authoritarian as well. Whether the biblical understanding of the "kingdom of God" is hierarchical is a separate question; in the chapter on process hermeneutics we shall give an example of why we think it is not necessarily so. Here, however, we are discussing the tradition of classical theism. Clearly the traditional metaphors encourage us to think of God as the ultimate "strong male"—wholly active, controlling, independent, unemotional, inflexible, and utterly devoid of receptiveness, responsiveness, or sympathy. This strong male king, absolute, unchangeable, and passionless, was also the final judge of our lives, but not one who would judge empathetically. And, because God was thought to be not only all-powerful but also omniscient and omnibeneficent, God was also the "sanctioner of the status quo."[28] Simply put, if God has all the power, then the only possible conclusion is that the way things are is the way God wants or allows them to be. Any attempt at change or liberation is an impossible uphill battle against omnipotence.

New Metaphors for God

The new model for God which has been briefly outlined here calls for new metaphors. The relation between metaphors and models has been the subject of much discussion. Two extreme positions on their relation might be characterized as follows. One holds that all we ever have are metaphors, that models are merely metaphors with "staying power."[29] Further, "a metaphor is a word or phrase used *in*appropriately. It belongs properly in one context but is being used in another: the arm of the chair, war as a chess game, God the father."[30] Hence metaphor is an improper language that refers to its object "only through a detour." Models are simply metaphors that have gained wide acceptance and have been around a long time, but which as metaphors are no more appropriate than any other metaphors.

The other position, at the opposite extreme, is the emotive theory of metaphor, adopted by a few logical positivist philosophers. It holds that metaphorical statements are not capable of verification by sense experience (how could we possibly know that "time is a child at play"?), and therefore are not genuinely meaningful statements. The only difference, therefore, between metaphors and nonsense phrases (such as, "when the Absolute falls into the water, it becomes a fish") is that metaphors have or evoke powerful emotive meanings in those who entertain them. But they have no cognitive meaning, which is reserved to strictly literal statements.[31]

Rather than try to settle this matter here (which would take us somewhat astray from the purpose of articulating the relationship between process theology and preaching), we will state that we see no good reason to subjugate either metaphors or concepts to one another. The emotive theory of metaphor, which regards metaphor as mere window dressing on a genuine idea, denies that there is any cognitive content to metaphor, which is surely an unreasonable position to take. The theory of metaphor according to which metaphor is all there is denies that there is any cognitive content to concepts or models, which seems equally unreasonable. Also it runs the risk, in its claim that everything is metaphor, of denying that anything is metaphor. The very term "metaphor" gains its meaning by contrast with terms such as "literal." The position of Frank Burch Brown, that in every metaphor something is obscured and in every concept something is lost, seems more promising than alternatives that would reduce either metaphors or models to each other.[32] Many concepts or models are indeed generated from metaphors, and perhaps all of them are. In that sense, McFague may be right that models are metaphors with "staying power." But it is also the case, as many students of Whitehead have discovered for themselves, that the power generated by his use of several unconventional metaphors for God—metaphors introduced at the *end* of a long and sustained metaphysical analysis—is possible only because these metaphors are introduced subsequent to that analysis. Then these metaphors themselves are powerful, in fresh new ways in which, beforehand, they would not have been.

The new model for God that has been briefly outlined here calls for new metaphors. Models are inherently abstract. While they may constitute a great gain in clarity, they lack concrete and symbolic richness. While it is clarifying to say that God is the one individual who interacts with all others, the one subject who knows all others and is known by all others (even if not all others know God *as* God), this remains a highly abstract way of talking. For this reason, process thinkers as well as other theologians have also sought to develop new metaphors for God, to which we now turn.

The World as God's Body

Among process thinkers, the first to propose that we think of the world as God's body was Charles Hartshorne. He suggested that we use the analogy of the relation between the body and the mind or self as a way of thinking about the relation between the world and God. As the human mind interacts with the nerve cells and molecules of the body, Hartshorne submits "that each creature is to God somewhat as a nerve cell is to us."[33] Of course, an analogy involves not only similarity but difference, and in this case one difference is that whereas our bodies have external environments, God has no external environment—because every creature is "in" God's experience. Another difference is that whereas we are imperfectly aware of our bodies, God is perfectly aware of God's body.

Process theologians have not been slow to pick up on Hartshorne's suggestion, as we saw earlier.[34] The analogy—self:body::God:world—has been widely used by them and been found attractive by theologians of nature. It is being looked upon favorably today even by more traditional theologians, who recognize that on the contemporary holistic understanding of persons as embodied, an embodied personal God is more appropriate to the Christian tradition and more credible than the classical view of a disembodied absolute.[35] More recently, however, Sallie McFague has developed the notion of the world as God's body in ways that are particularly helpful for Christians seeking to think and act responsibly in our nuclear-ecological age.[36]

Here we want to suggest why preachers should give serious consideration to thinking of the world as God's body as they set out to teach the Christian faith in our time. First, as McFague argues, Christians have "a surprisingly 'bodily' tradition."[37] The resurrection and ascension of Jesus Christ can be understood as God's promise "to be permanently present, 'bodily' present to us, in all times and places of our world."[38] The church has been understood as the *body* of Christ who is its head; the eucharist has been understood as the body and blood of Christ. Why should we not at least experiment with thinking of the world as God's body? Certainly the idea is less incredible and less inappropriate than thinking of God as disembodied. Nor does using this metaphor "reduce" God to the world, any more than we are "reduced" to our bodies.

Second, if the world is God's body, then in our nuclear-ecological age God is "at risk."[39] All our assaults upon the world—destroying its arable land; polluting its air, water, and soil; simplifying its ecosystems; threatening the elimination of virtually all its life through nuclear warfare—are also assaults upon God. As harming a human being's body harms the person as well, so to injure the world is to injure God. Similarly as we are morally responsible to care for our bodies, so "God cares about the world as one cares about one's body."[40] The metaphor of the world as God's body not only declares God's sympathetic caring for the world, but discloses God's love of embodiment, thus reversing the long anti-body, anti-physical tradition that allowed Christianity to suppress women, ignore the earth, and accuse Jews of "carnality."

Third, sin and responsibility are redefined in the metaphor of the world as God's body. Sin as pride or *hubris* now is regarded as the refusal to be part of the world, the only part we can be, finite and responsible agents. Sin is against this-world-in-God, not merely against God or other people. To sin is "to refuse to take responsibility for nurturing, loving, and befriending the body and all its parts."[41] Sin is the pride that denies our interdependence with life in all its forms. Similarly, the ethics of the world/God metaphor is one that directs us to care for, protect, and befriend the world itself as if God's very vulnerability were in our keeping. If God does, indeed, feel with all the creatures all of their feelings, then it is true that whatever we do to even the least of these, we do to God, as the parable of the Last Judgment reminds us.

There is good reason to recommend the metaphor of the world as God's body to those who would teach and proclaim the Christian witness in our time. The traditional model was largely silent on the subject of the nonhuman world, and in its hierarchical and monarchical articulation encouraged attitudes supportive of coercive force, dualism, otherworldliness, and escapism. Such attitudes are not conducive to helping Christians deal responsibly with the systemic injustices of our time, with racism, sexism, classism, terracide (the killing of the environment), and militarism. The metaphor of the world as God's body inspires attitudes of care for the vulnerable and oppressed, care for the earth, and affirmation of the body. It sets forth in fresh terms the promise of the love of God for each and all and the command of God that justice be done to each and all. It is appropriate to the Christian faith and of practical, moral help in our nuclear-ecological age—particularly if the preacher's task is, as we believe, to articulate the Christian faith in ways that are morally credible and that affirm the gracious love and commanding justice of God.

God as Companion

Over half a century ago, Alfred North Whitehead criticized the model of God in traditional Christian theology for its monarchical character: "He stood in the same relation to the whole World as early Egyptian or Mesopotamian kings stood to their subject populations."[42] God was necessary to the world, but the world was in no sense necessary to God. Because the theologians of the formative period of church history retained such images of God, they failed to deal adequately with what had been revealed in Christ about the nature of God and God's way of acting in the world.[43]

Thus it was, according to Whitehead, that when Christianity became established, "Caesar conquered."[44] In spite of the fact that the Galilean origin of Christianity "dwells upon the tender elements of the world, which slowly and in quietness operate by love," the church continued to fashion "God in the image of the Egyptian, Persian, and Roman imperial rulers."[45] It "gave unto God the attributes which belonged exclusively to Caesar." God was modeled as the "unmoved mover" of Aristotle, as an imperial ruler, or as relentless moral energy. Yet "love," says Whitehead, "neither rules, nor is it unmoved; also it is a little oblivious to morals."[46]

Because he thought that "the nature of God is dipolar,"[47] Whitehead argued that there is another aspect to the activity by which God creates the world.[48] This other aspect he called God's "consequent nature," by virtue of which what happens in the world passes into the life of God where the flux and transience of finitude become permanent. The consequent nature expresses the gentleness of God, the "tender care that nothing be lost."[49] This is God in God's role of redeemer of the world, redeeming it by suffering with it and granting it meaning and worth beyond itself.

In this way Whitehead came up with a new metaphor for God, that of God as "the great *companion*—the fellow-sufferer who understands."[50] God as companion or friend is our second major metaphor for God. Although it has not been typical of Christians to speak of God as "companion," neither has it been entirely foreign to our tradition. Many free-church Protestants grew up singing the hymn, "What a friend we have in Jesus," in which Jesus, clearly standing as a theologoumenon for God, bears all our sins and griefs. The word *companion* is derived from the Latin *cum* (with) and *panis* (bread). A companion shares the same table with you, breaks bread with you, befriends you. When Christians celebrate "the breaking of bread," they are responding to God's invitation to be friends of God, of each other, of the world, of the Friend of the world.

The metaphor of God as the great or unfailing companion is more appropriate to the gospel of God's freely offered love than is that of the ruling despot (*despotes* is the Greek word for "all-powerful") and more helpful to us in our post-Holocaust, nuclear world. The origin of Christian worship in the table-fellowship participated in by Jesus and his disciples, and the inclusive character of these fellowships as attested to in the earliest Christian witness, proclaim a dramatic theological point: God wants to break bread with us, to be our companion on the way of life that is faith.

In an essay on the Holy Spirit, David Burrell makes this metaphor the central theme of his work, pointing out that, in John's gospel, when Jesus calls us to follow him we are "invited to become his friends." This invitation to friendship with divinity signals God's "delight in being with us," and "creates an entirely new dimension of receptivity in us."[51] Hence the term "spirit" articulates both God's intention to be related to us and voices our capacity, as transformed by God's grace, "to be related intentionally to all things."[52] So the core metaphor for the new life granted by the Spirit is "friendship with God."[53]

To be related intentionally to "all things" means that we must relate adequately to the earth itself. The rabbinic commentaries on the Genesis creation stories stress that God entrusted everything God made to those of us, female and male, who were created in God's image; the most appropriate image for the friends of God who would continue creation by caring for it is "stewardship."[54] Socially and politically, to be intentionally related to all things as friends of

God is to seek to do justice toward all those whom God loves. Concern with justice for women, ethnic minorities, the poor, and the alien others of oppressive ideologies will lead us to work for genuine freedom and equality for the neighbor. In this way are we friends of God.

Sallie McFague suggests that God's friendly love of the creatures is God's liking them: "A friend is someone you like and someone who likes you."[55] A friend is one with whom you share a common vision and care about a common truth: "Friendship with God in our time can be seen as focused on a common project: the salvation, the well-being of the earth."[56] And, friendship is an adult relationship in which we must be willing "to grow up and take responsibility for the world."[57] To do so is the only appropriate response for those who are friends of the Friend of the world.

Yet such responsibility is wearying, which is where the grace of the Friend plays its role. One breaks bread with the Friend, and bread is nourishing. When Whitehead introduced the metaphor of God as companion, he claimed that God is the source of "refreshment."[58] Hence the love of God as friend is a sustaining love.[59] The witness of the early church is to an inclusive table-fellowship on the part of Jesus, testifying to the all-inclusiveness of God's sustaining love. God is friend of all and calls us to befriend all.

God as Mother

The new model of God as genuinely related to and caring about the world, as engaged in pathos with and struggle for it, also encourages us to consider seriously another metaphor for God, one espoused by feminists: that of God as mother. One of the difficulties with all our models and metaphors is that sometimes we forget they are just that—models and metaphors which are not God but which point to God. When we forget this, we literalize our models and metaphors (particularly the familiar ones), and we are persnickety about doing this with such inherited models of God as king, father, and impassible absolute. Neither do new models and metaphors do anything more than point to that which both transcends and undercuts them. Yet these new models can help relativize the old ones and alert us to the reality of God's grace in fresh and helpful ways.

With regard to the metaphor of God as mother, the Christian tradition has more resources on which to draw than is the case with other metaphors. First, there is the tradition of the negative theology, which reminds us that all our ways of speaking of God are fallible, that none of them literally names God. It is the merit of this tradition that it applied its insight to the name "father." In his early third-century apology, the *Octavius*, Minucius Felix, a North African churchman, defended the church against the standard battery of charges that the apologists attributed to their pagan critics. Some of these charges centered around alleged sexual excesses in Christian worship involving the male priest. Partly in order to combat such accusations and partly to affirm the transcendence of God, Minucius argued against calling God "father."

Minucius contended that "God" is the only name for God, that the name "father" encourages pagans to think of God as "earthly," the name "king" suggests that God is "carnal," and the name "Lord" indicates that God is mortal.[60] Father also suggests maleness, a connotation that Minucius sought to avoid. In its place he argued that God is more appropriately called "parent." God is the "parent of the universe," the "parent of all," the "parent of the world" as Plato understood, and the parent of all people who are brothers of each other.[61] Although Minucius did not say "brothers and sisters of each other," it may be anachronistic to criticize him for not having done so. Nor should we dismiss Minucius as a minor aberration in Christian thought. The tendency to speak of God as parent was not confined to him but was somewhat widespread among Latin-speaking Christians in North Africa. For example, we have the hymn "Of the Father's Love Begotten," taken from the writings of Aurelius Prudentius Clemens, a contemporary of Augustine. The Latin first line of the hymn reads: *Corde natus ex Parentis*, "Of the Parent's Love Begotten." This hymn reflects an instance when a nineteenth-century translation renders our tradition more sexist than it already was.

As feminist scholars have pointed out, we also have more resources in the biblical tradition than we remember. The mystery of God's freedom as the scriptures witness to it obviously transcends the biological distinctions between male and female, as it does the cultural distinctions of masculine and feminine. Not only does the self-revelation of God to Moses in Exodus 3 point to a metaphor of God as "helper," but in Genesis 2, when Eve is said to have been created as the "helper" of Adam, the biblical tradition uses for Eve a word, "help," that, according to Samuel Terrien, "is generally applied to God who is par excellence the succor of those in need and despair."[62] Hence Adam and Eve, created together in God's image, are theomorphic in their co-humanity and are given the responsibility to care for the rest of creation as God's helpers.

The image of God as a mother bird is present in scripture: "Hide me in the shadow of your wings" (Psalm 17:8); "All people may take refuge in the shadow of your wings" (Psalm 36:7); "in the shadow of your wings I will take refuge" (Psalm 57:1); "Like birds hovering overhead, so the LORD of hosts will protect Jerusalem" (Isaiah 31:5). Although this language is made to refer to the Lord, it is "likely drawn from the representation of female goddesses with *sheltering wings*," protecting their young.[63] Matthew 23:37 and Luke 13:34 attribute to Jesus the statement about Jerusalem: "How often have I desired to gather your children together as a hen gathers her brood under her wings, and you were not willing!" Sadly, this latter passage has been taken up into the church's anti-Jewish tradition, and has not been allowed to express its message of God's all-inclusive love.

Names and images of God as *wife* or *mother* also appear. In Psalm 51 the Psalmist appeals to God's motherly compassion, and the love of God is compared with a mother's love for her child or a wife's affection for her husband (e.g., Psalm 131:2, Psalm 49:14–15). "You forgot the God who gave you birth," declares Deuteronomy 32:18. The Hebraic tradition used several names in the feminine gender for God: *Shekinah*, to refer to the all-present One, *Torah* to refer to God's teaching for us, *Chokmah* to name God's wisdom. The "spirit" of God, *ruach*, is feminine. Some of these names—notably *sophia*, wisdom—retain their feminine gender in the Christian tradition, although *sophia* is gradually replaced by *logos*.

The image of God as mother should not replace that of God as father; rather, the two should be used together and in alteration with each other. Father is, after all, also a parental metaphor, and God is not literally either father or mother. Strictly speaking, God loves in ways appropriate to God's categorically unique status, which is to say that God loves as only God can love. God loves each and all and does so perfectly. Fathers and mothers love as fathers and mothers love, and do so imperfectly (as those of us who are fathers or mothers know only too well). Nor should we sentimentalize the love of mothers for their children, or disparage that of fathers. Either can fail drastically. The point is to de-literalize and de-stabilize inherited metaphors so that in our thought and speech God is freed to be God, to be understood to love in ways that include but transcend male and female.

The metaphor of God as female or mother (not all female metaphors of God are maternal, as we have seen) helps us to stress the all-inclusiveness of God's love. We saw this in Minucius Felix's insistence that God is parent of all and of all the world, in the emphasis in *Shekinah* on God as the all-present One, in the mother bird who struggles to protect the life of all her children. "God as the giver of life, as the power of being in all being, can be imaged through the metaphor of mother—and of father."[64] The nurturing, sustaining love of God, also seen in the metaphor of God as companion, is reinforced by God as mother who feeds her children. Because God as mother loves all her children and has more than merely human ones, love of God as mother entails working for justice for our sisters and brothers as well as for the ecosystem as such.

Conclusion

Throughout this discussion the underlying motif has been what Karl Barth called "the freedom of God," God's freedom to be with us and for us.[65] The point and purpose of suggesting new models and metaphors for God is to free us up sufficiently from the old ones, and particularly from a literalizing understanding of them, to enable us to speak today of God's love and justice in ways that are appropriate to the Christian tradition but also credible in our situation. With such new models, preachers will be better able to address the urgent issues of our time in ways that command the attention of thoughtful people.

Notes

[1]Bernard E. Meland, *Fallible Forms and Symbols* (Philadelphia: Fortress Press, 1976).

[2]Langdon Gilkey, "God," in *Christian Theology: An Introduction to Its Traditions and Tasks*, ed. Peter C. Hodgson and Robert H. King (Philadelphia:

Fortress Press, 1985), p. 90.

[3]*Ibid.*, p. 93.

[4]*Ibid.*

[5]Clement of Alexandria, *Miscellanies*, Vol. 5, in *Documents in Early Christian Thought*, ed. Maurice Wiles and Mark Santer (Cambridge: Cambridge University Press, 1975), pp. 4-7.

[6]*Ibid.*, p. 6.

[7]*Ibid.*, p. 7.

[8]Origen, *Homilies on Jeremiah 18:7-10*, in *Documents in Early Christian Thought*, p. 7.

[9]*Ibid.*, p. 10.

[10]Augustine, *On the Psalms 134:3-6*, in *Documents in Early Christian Thought*, p. 18.

[11]*Ibid.*, p. 19.

[12]Anselm, "The Attributes of God," in *Readings in Christian Theology*, ed. Peter C. Hodgson and Robert H. King (Philadelphia: Fortress Press, 1985), p. 66.

[13]Anselm, *Basic Writings*, tr. S. N. Deane (LaSalle, IL: Open Court, 1962), p. 13.

[14]Russell Pregeant, *Mystery Without Magic* (Oak Park, IL: Meyer-Stone Books, 1988), p. 107.

[15]John Calvin, "God's Providence Governs All," in *Readings in Christian Theology*, ed. Hodgson and King, p. 124.

[16]Whitehead, *Process and Reality*, p. 342f.

[17]*Ibid.*, p. 343.

[18]Schubert M. Ogden, *The Reality of God* (New York: Harper & Row, 1966), p. 57.

[19]*Ibid.*

[20]*Ibid.*, p. 58.

[21]Charles Hartshorne, *The Divine Relativity* (New Haven: Yale University Press, 1948), p. 20.

[22]Ogden, *The Reality of God*, p. 60.

[23]Alfred North Whitehead, *Science and the Modern World* (New York: The New American Library, 1925), p. 160.

[24]This set of changes is in accord with Whitehead's ontological principle "that actual entities are the only *reasons*; so that to search for a *reason* is to search for one or more actual entities." See *Process and Reality*, p. 24.

[25]John B. Cobb, Jr., *Talking About God* [with David Tracy] (New York: The Seabury Press, 1983), p. 53.

[26]Schubert M. Ogden, "The Metaphysics of Faith and Justice," *Process Studies*, Vol. 14 (Summer 1985), p. 96.

[27]Charles Hartshorne, *The Divine Relativity*, p. 152.

[28]John B. Cobb, Jr. and David R. Griffin, *Process Theology: An Introductory Exposition* (Philadelphia: Westminster Press, 1976), p. 9.

[29]This is the position of Sallie McFague, *Models of God* (Philadelphia: Fortress Press, 1987), p. 34.

[30]*Ibid.*, p. 33.

[31]The emotive theory of metaphor is expressed by M. Rieser, "Brief Introduction to the Epistemology of Art," *Journal of Philosophy*, Vol. 47 (1950), pp. 695-704.

[32]Frank Burch Brown, "Transfiguration: Poetic Metaphor and Theological Reflection," *The Journal of Religion*, Vol. 62 (Jan. 1982), p. 56. Our statement in the text is a very concise summary of Brown's sophisticated and nuanced position which he presents more fully in *Transfiguration* (Chapel Hill: University of North Carolina Press, 1983).

[33]Charles Hartshorne, *A Natural Theology for Our Time* (LaSalle, IL: Open Court, 1966), p. 97f.

[34]Ogden, *The Reality of God*, p. 60.

[35]Grace Jantzen, *God's World, God's Body* (Philadelphia: Westminster Press, 1984), chap. 3.

[36]McFague, *Models of God*, pp. 69-78.

[37]*Ibid.*, p. 71.

[38]*Ibid.*, p. 60.

[39]*Ibid.*, p. 72.

[40]*Ibid.*, p. 73.

[41]*Ibid.*, p. 77.

[42]Alfred North Whitehead, *Adventures of Ideas* (New York: Macmillan, 1933), p. 169.

[43]*Ibid.*, p. 167.

[44]Whitehead, *Process and Reality*, p. 342.

[45]*Ibid.*

[46]*Ibid.*, p. 343.

[47]*Ibid.*, p. 345.

[48]*Ibid.*, p. 343.

[49]*Ibid.*, p. 346.

[50]*Ibid.*, p. 351; emphasis ours.

[51]David B. Burrell, "The Spirit and the Christian Life," in *Christian Theology: Its Traditions and Tasks*, p. 302.

[52]*Ibid.*, p. 303.

[53]*Ibid.*, p. 306.

[54]*Ibid.*, p. 323.

[55]McFague, *Models of God*, p. 160.

[56]*Ibid.*, p. 163.

[57]*Ibid.*, p. 165.

[58]Whitehead, *Process and Reality*, p. 351.

[59]McFague, *Models of God*, p. 167ff.

[60]Minucius Felix, *Octavius*, in *The Ante-Nicene Fathers*, Vol. IV, ed. Alexander Roberts and James Donaldson (Grand Rapids: Eerdmans, 1979), p. 183.

[61]*Ibid.*, pp. 182-184.

[62]Cited in Letty Russell, *Human Liberation in a Feminist Perspective— A Theology* (Philadelphia: Westminster Press, 1974), p. 99.

[63]*Ibid.*, p. 100.

[64]McFague, *Models of God*, p. 103.

[65]Karl Barth, *The Humanity of God*, tr. J. N. Thomas and T. Weiser (Richmond: John Knox Press, 1960), p. 48.

Chapter

Preaching and Systemic Injustice

The Sounds of Silence

An impression of preaching today is that preachers seldom deal with the major structural evils of our time. Most preaching is oriented to the lectionary and takes an exegetical approach to texts. Most lectionaries are oriented to the Christian year, which means that most of the Old Testament—a multi-splendored book that deals with politics and kings, rogues and prostitutes, Israel's covenantal responsibility toward the environment and the covenant with all the creatures made with Noah, the rise and fall of empires—is sliced and diced and made to fit the story of the life of Jesus.[1] Yet this is hardly the whole problem. The typical interpretation given to texts in "mainline" churches is psychological, and the chief application made of them is to the more personal and private aspects of life. Insofar as contemporary theology attends to fundamental moral questions, as it does in the various theologies of liberation, these theologies seem to make little impact on the pulpit. Perhaps they are wrongly seen merely as voicing the concerns of people other than the predominantly middle-class folk who occupy the pews.

When major structural evils are addressed or mentioned, the manner in which they are treated is often less than satisfactory. Sometimes the hearer receives only a vague sense of what the preacher's position on the issue is, and even less often are hearers helped to think through the issue from a Christian point of view. Perhaps this is because preachers themselves are honestly puzzled about how to do just that. Perhaps it is because preachers fear the consequences of preaching a de-privatized gospel to a comfortable congregation. Perhaps it is because the clergy reward system in churches and judicatories provides no pay-off for ministers who do not "play it safe."

This impressionistic sense is backed up by research. In 1968, a team of sociologists asked 1,580 Protestant clergy, selected at random from California churches, what kind of sermons they had given in the preceding year. That year had been one of the most tortured in American history, having witnessed the assassinations of Martin Luther King, Jr., and Robert Kennedy, the burning of dozens of American cities, the issuance of the Kerner Commission report on racism, the Tet offensive in Vietnam, the six-day war in the Mideast, the withdrawal of Lyndon Johnson from the presidential campaign, and the starvation of tens of thousands of Biafrans in Africa.

In such a tumultuous year of moral chaos, one might expect volumes of commentary from the pulpit. This was not the case. Instead, only 6 percent of the sermons preached spoke substantially to social and political issues.[2] Moreover, most preachers who dealt with such questions did so only in passing. They "touched upon" social questions far more than they "mainly devoted" sermons to them. When major issues were referred to, they were treated peripherally. The manner in which they were touched upon was "in bland, ambiguous, and vague ways."[3] Apparently, when preachers do mention controversy, the trend is to do so without being controversial, to speak circumspectly. The tendency to pulpit silence is so strong that not even the Tet offensive or the sight of American cities in flames could induce a third of the clergy to break their silence on political questions.[4] Although race relations were on the front burner (so to speak) in 1968, 55 percent of California pulpits were silent on the topic. While Watts burned, only 7 percent of the sermons delivered had *anything* to say about Black Power, and only 22 percent dealt with national poverty. World poverty was more interesting (28 percent). An attempt in California to repeal an open housing law was met with silence in 44 percent of the churches.

Nor is it the case that the above conclusions are wrong by virtue of being based on an outdated study. Two 1988 studies of clergy in the Christian Church (Disciples of Christ) came to essentially the same conclusions. One, drawing on the self-reports of 90 percent of Disciples senior ministers who participated, indicates that these pastors are most reluctant to address their congregations precisely on those issues where they perceive the greatest gap between them and their congregations.[5] The other, based on a careful reading of 206 sermons randomly selected from a larger number submitted, contends that, in general, Disciples preachers in 1988 simply did not address major social-ethical issues.[6]

Conclude the sociologists: "It is as if there had been no Sermon on the Mount."[7] It is apparently not the case that laypeople hear sermons articulating Christian approaches to major issues, but remain deaf to what they hear. Rather is it that laypeople "cannot be blamed for ignoring sermons that were not preached."[8] The theological root of silence lies in the assumption on the part of preachers that the chief function of a sermon is to comfort the distressed. When this is accompanied by an otherworldly understanding of salvation and a privatized definition of sin, neither has anything to do with social and political issues or being redeemed by God's grace to work for the liberation of the neighbor. Also, these assumptions lead to a "miraculous view of social reform," the idea that if enough people come to Christ, social evils will disappear.[9] Hence, social evils themselves need not be addressed. Such a view ignores the fact that born-again Christians, like the rest of us, remain noticeably sinful.

Factors other than theological ones, of course, influence the clergy toward silence on serious issues. Congregations seldom pass out rewards for the "most courageous sermon of the year." Many clergy are convinced that their congregations object to relevant sermons. Yet because some clergy do preach such sermons, it is hard to avoid the conclusion that when the pulpit is silent, the silence is self-imposed.

Addressing Systemic Injustice

Perhaps it will strengthen our resolve to break through the sounds of silence if we look again at what preaching is. To preach is to teach the Christian faith. As a definition, this looks like a simple and straightforward matter. All a preacher has to do is to learn what the Christian faith is and then teach it to other people. Complicating the situation, however, is the fact that we are always called upon to teach the Christian faith to people who live in a new historical situation, one significantly different from that in which those people were born. Preachers must speak plausibly to questions that are not only urgent but new, if they are to help people understand what it means to live a Christian life in the present.

Further complicating the task of preaching is the other side of this same fact: that the Christian faith must itself be reinterpreted by those who would be freed by it to speak to new and urgent questions. The forms taken in the past by the Christian tradition, while they may have been adequate for their times, do not always speak helpfully to a drastically changed situation. For example, what those of us born before World War II learned of the Christian faith in our childhood does not address adequately the world in which we must now live our adult lives. The world of our childhood was before Hiroshima and Nagasaki, before Auschwitz and Theresienstadt, before smog and acid rain, as well as before our consciousness had been raised about women's issues, anti-Juda-ism, militarism, issues of economic exploitation, cultural oppres-sion, and bureaucratic manipulation. It is obvious that if we are to pass on the Christian faith to people today, we cannot do so simply by repeating it. If we are to help people understand the world in which they live in the light of the Christian faith, we must also help them understand the Christian faith in the light of questions arising from the world in which they live.

If Christian proclamation is to be a vital source of faith and life, rather than a means of evading faith and escaping life, it must be reinterpreted in order to speak helpfully to each new situation, thereby helping people understand as well the situation in which they are called and claimed to live as Christians. Anyone possessing a cursory familiarity with the history of the church recognizes that, in fact, the Christian tradition remained vital precisely because it was reinterpreted from epoch to epoch. There is no "absolute" core to the Christian faith that endures through time unchanged. It does not consist of a husk underneath which lies a kernel that, after we have dug it out, can serve as the locus of absolute authority for our day. Rather, as John B. Cobb argues, Christian faith must be seen as a living whole which, because it is living, "is in constant change."[10] Says Cobb of the question of the interpretation of scripture:

> The theological task is not only to interpret given texts, but also to find the texts which are relevant in different times and places....We study our scriptures as participants in the Christian movement seeking to respond faithfully to the challenges of our time. Our identity depends on our rootedness. But a healthy identity depends on our willing- ness to confess the many crimes which our movement has committed.[11]

The more drastic the change from one era to another, the more far-reaching the reinterpretation that is demanded. Process theol- ogy—particularly in its hermeneutical stress that texts can come to mean something different from and more than they have ever meant before—encourages us to engage in the faithful and critical conver- sation between the systemic evils characteristic of our late twenti- eth-century world and the dangerous memories embedded in the texts at the root of our movement.

Process Theology and Systemic Evils

We saw above some of the theological commitments that make dealing with systemic injustices particularly difficult for preachers: a privatized definition of sin, an individualistic otherworldly view of salvation, and a miraculous understanding of social reform. The first two presuppose an understanding of persons or individuals as essentially unrelated both to one another and to the larger nonhuman environment. The third makes the same presupposition; if individu- als change, the social context will take care of itself because it is made up of individuals who for utilitarian reasons "contract" to live together. The third fails to see that our relationships, the whole socioeconomic process in which we participate, goes into the making of individuals as much as individuals shape their relationships.

Ignoring systemic injustices also seems to reflect a view of God as the omnipotent wielder of the thunder who could, in a twinkling, make everything right if "he" so chose. That "he" does not do so apparently means that things are just fine as they are. Otherwise, would not God, knowing what is happening, being able to change it, and wanting to do good, rectify the situation? All the assumptions that underlie or could be used to rationalize keeping silent in the face of massive injustice are rejected by process theology.

God, as understood by process theology, is internally related to and affected by all of God's creatures. This does not mean that the being or character of God is altered by participating in relationships, but it does mean that God experiences perfectly the pains and joys of all God's creatures, great and small. That God "knows," empathetically and not just abstractly, my own joys and hurts, turmoil and confusion, is awesome to contemplate; God knows each of us better than we know ourselves, better than we can know ourselves. God is directly affected by all our deeds and misdeeds, by what we do and fail to do on behalf of the neighbor or stranger in need, want, and pain. Christians have long lived with the impossible tension between a God who has been thought to be utterly immutable, incapable of being affected by anything which happens to the creatures, and the revelation of that same God in Christ who said that "as you did it to one of the least of these...you did it to me" (Matthew 25:40). Here the traditional doctrine of God undercuts the revelatory power of Jesus Christ. Process theology's doctrine of God is appropriate to and interprets that same revelation; also it gives us no excuse for ignoring systemic injustice practiced against anyone.

Nor does process theology support the understanding of human beings as isolated individuals unrelated to, not affected by, and not affecting their larger environment in its social and natural aspects. Individuals were thought of traditionally as independent substances, in no important ways related to their social and environmental context, enduring through time unchanged. Even here the logical import of some definitions of "substance," such as Descartes', could have been blunted by experience and common sense. Nonetheless, just such a view of the person as unrelated individual, or as related only to a small and comparatively private nuclear family, underlies the notion that we are saved one by one, not *with* but *in spite of* and *out of* our circumstances and relationships. The impact on Christianity of gnostic and docetic understandings of human beings and salvation—that people are saved individually from this dirty, carnal world to a better one on high—has been much more profound than histories of Christian thought admit. The process theological understanding of human beings stresses that the person is an individual/social reciprocal. In one sense, we are precisely the individuals we are because of the distinctive set of social relationships in which we participate and which go into the making of us. No one else had parents like mine. Even different children in one family do not strictly have the "same" parents. The oldest child may have grown up in a home with young parents, little money, and younger siblings, while the youngest child was part of a family with middle-aged parents, adequate money, and older siblings. These two children lived in very different families. In another sense, the reason in process thought why we have to "decide" how to understand and constitute ourselves is not, as in some forms of existentialism, because we are ontologically alone but precisely because so much and so many go into the making of us. If we were not to decide what influences were more important or valuable, we would wind up simply as a junk heap of other people's donations to our experience. But other people and other members of the environment are part of us, as we are of them. Because of this relational nature of human beings, it is deceptive to talk of salvation as individualistic, as if any one of us could find health when so many to whom we are internally related do not.

Neither sin nor salvation can be appropriately or credibly interpreted as merely pertaining to isolated individuals. The strongest point of the traditional doctrine of original sin was its clear awareness of the sociohistorical character of sin. The past goes into the making of the present. Somehow, willy-nilly, we must take it into account and take responsibility, not for what people once did long ago but for what we now will do with what they have left us. At the same time we are trying to cope with the difficulty that how we have been shaped by what has been "given" to us is who we are as we try to struggle with the burden of donated evil.

Nor are any of our own sins merely private; indeed, there is no purely private experience. All the ways in which we fail to respond to God's calling of us forward are ways in which our failures and ambiguities go into the making not only of our future selves but of all those others who are or will be affected by us. Sin is never purely private or unconnected with systemic injustices.

Uncomfortable as it may be to consider, much light is shed on systemic injustice when we ask the simple question: "Who profits from this? Who benefits?" Males benefit from sexism. Whites benefit from racism. Christians benefit from anti-Judaism. European and American consumers and investors benefit from corporations doing business in South Africa. Land developers and builders benefit, temporarily, from the rape of the countryside. Automobile manufacturers and oil companies benefit from smog, as do highway construction companies. Tobacco companies and their stockholders benefit from the sale of poisons which people "voluntarily" consume. The social-relational character of evil becomes obvious when we ask who gets the payoff from it.

In spite of process theology's quite correct insistence that there is no absolute unchanging essence of Christianity that endures throughout the ages, we do think that a norm of appropriateness can be stated and used to criticize current and inadequate interpretations of the Christian faith. This norm, as we have argued elsewhere, can be derived from the canonical criticism of James A. Sanders, who, in turn, derives it from the self-correcting hermeneutic of scripture understood as a process of the interpretation and reinterpretation of the biblical tradition across almost two millennia of changing contexts of biblical history and over five different cultural eras.[12] This norm, taken as the word of God or the gospel, is the promise of the love of God graciously offered to each and all, and the command of God that justice be done to each and all of those whom God loves.

Differing somewhat from some process theologians, we find that it is precisely because new interpretations of the Christian faith are so creative and innovative that we need a norm of appropriateness for looking critically at new interpretations. The reason we mention this here is because, in our judgment, what it will take to free and encourage preachers to speak the liberating word of God's grace and judgment to a generation wallowing in systemic injustice, to break their silence on "the weightier matters of the law" (Matthew 23:23), is precisely an understanding of the gospel as it is addressed to ourselves. When and if we recognize that the only ultimate way in which we may authentically decide to understand ourselves is in terms of and only in terms of God's gracious love for us, then will we be freed from all those misunderstandings that keep us silent. We will cease seeking safety in silence when we realize that God's love, which commands our love of God and the neighbor in return, is the only final ground of our ultimate safety, the perfect love that casts out fear—even fear of the congregation.

Here we turn to sketch, in broad outline, five of the systemic injustices to which preachers and teachers of the Christian faith ought increasingly to address themselves. With regard to each one we indicate some of the resources available in process theology for responding to it.

Five Systemic Injustices

A systemic issue is one that affects an entire system, somewhat as a serious disease, such as cancer, affects the entire bodily system of a human being. A systemic injustice is not one problem among others. It is a problem affecting all members of a system and the system as a whole. Thus, all systemic evils are interrelated with one another and each of them affects both every human being and the earth itself.

One is the unjust exploitation of nature in its biological, zoological, physical, and chemical dimensions. The whole ecosystem, in which human beings participate and which sustains human life, is itself under threat. We will call this ecological threat *homocentrism*, the view that only human beings are of value and only they are to be saved. Another is the unjust distribution of goods and services favoring a wealthy minority of groups and classes and exploiting the labor and lives of the majority of people on the planet. We will call this systemic evil *classism*, since it involves the oppression and exploitation of one socioeconomic class by another. A third systemic evil is *sexism*, the deep and prevalent oppression both of women and of all those dependent on women, mainly children and the elderly. A fourth systemic evil is *racism*, the repression of millions of people who, in particular places, belong to ethnic groups that are dominated by other ethnic groups in those places. In America the victims of racism, chiefly, are blacks, Native Americans, and Hispanic Americans, but every ethnic group, at one time or another, has known what it means to be marginalized. *Militarism*, the violent use of force to defend a system of unjust relationships, is the fifth systemic injustice. There is internal militarism, whereby injustice within a nation is defended by the military, and external militarism, the violent expropriation of power outside a given nation resulting in oppression. Sometimes two evils collide, as when a corrupt internal militarism is taken over by an external corrupt militarism; one doesn't know for which side to root. The ultimate form of militarism is the *nuclear threat*, which is also the ultimate form of *homocentrism*, the threat to the environment, which coincidence demonstrates the interrelatedness of the systemic injustices.

These systemic injustices can be said to give our age in human history its distinctive character. Auschwitz and Hiroshima stand near the middle of our century as powerful symbols, powerful because they are more than symbols, of the fact that human evil respects no limits or restraints upon its plans; evil is self-transcendent in pursuit of its goals and will always find an organizing principle. We live in what Sallie McFague calls the "ecological-nuclear age," a shorthand phrase handy for referring to the whole complex of systemic evils as well as their far-reaching capacity for destructiveness.[13] We have a power over the fate of the earth unlike people have ever before possessed. We need a theology that helps people understand that they are empowered to do more in the face of such extreme systemic evil than resign in despair or retreat into otherworldly salvation, the popularity of which is so great because it is so *tempting*. We need preaching that helps people live authentic Christian lives in this nuclear-ecological age. We need churches that do more than draw a curtain between congregants and the terrors of history.

The Whole Creation Groans in Travail

Almost every issue of the daily newspaper in any large city carries information about the threat to planet Earth. In banner headlines, we are alerted to the impending disasters with which the earth itself is faced—what one columnist calls "a grotesquely overdeveloped and corrupted ecosystem that threatens the survival, not only of whales and rhinos, but of the two-legged animals who are the culprits."[14] Ninety-seven percent of the Brazilian rain forest, source of much of the world's oxygen, has been lost to farms and cities since Europeans came to Brazil in the 1500s. A swath of rain forest as large as the state of Indiana is destroyed every day in the tropical world. As many as one-fifth of all species of land animals are in danger of disappearing in fifty years.

Toxic chemicals find their way into the Great Lakes from as far away as Central America, leading environmentalists to recognize that "we're not controlling pollution, we're just pushing it around."[15] In addition to chemicals from factories, sewage plants, and harbors, at least half the pollutants in Lake Michigan are blown into it from thousands of different sources. Roughly 1,000 toxic compounds in the lake are killing birds and fish and are capable, eventually, of threatening human life. Because the lake is so deep, it takes about a century for it to refill itself with new water, rendering the problem even more difficult.

Awareness of environmental problems is not new. In A.D. 61, Seneca complained of "the stink of the smoke chimneys" of Rome; in 1257 Eleanor of Aquitaine left Nottingham to avoid "the undesirable smoke," and in 1661 John Evelyn described London's "hellist and dismal cloud of sea coal."[16] The "fertile crescent" of the ancient Near East, stretching from the Tigris and Euphrates to Egypt, is today a desert, due to hillside farming, overgrazing, and the removal of the forest which held the soil. The forests of Lebanon, which once produced the cedars used to construct the Temple in Jerusalem, are today barren and devoid of topsoil. Agricultural methods practiced by the Mayan Empire in Central America destroyed the soil, causing cities to be abandoned and the empire to disappear.

With the rise of modern science and technology, making possible highly efficient mechanized farming methods and rapid population growth, the ecological problem has been transformed into a crisis. While it is true that science and technology have also alerted us to the crisis and proposed ways to deal with certain aspects of it, it is clear that science and technology alone are powerless to solve it.

Some major ecological problems are the following. *Upsetting the balance of an ecosystem*: An example of the many forms which this can take is the 1930s "dust bowl," which was created in the American Midwest because farming methods and overgrazing destroyed the sod that held the soil. When a drought followed, the soil blew away. The same farming methods are predominant today and pursued even more efficiently with larger equipment; as a result the Midwest loses about two bushels of topsoil per year for every bushel of corn or wheat harvested. Destruction of land by farming methods, by cutting down trees for firewood, and by overgrazing threatens not only the land but people. Mass starvation in Ethiopia is related to the growth of the Sahara Desert, which expands by about 40,000 acres a year.[17]

Another is *air pollution*. Pollutants are the residues of things we use and throw away. Acid rain, destructive of forests, crops, trees and lakes, is the most well-publicized result of air pollution; in some parts of the world the rain is as acidic as Coca Cola.[18] The burning of fossil fuels, oil, natural gas, and coal increases the carbon dioxide content of the atmosphere, which in turn acts as a blanket reducing the amount of heat radiated at night, resulting in the "greenhouse effect." The consequent warming of the earth is predicted to bring about rising sea levels, threatening coastal cities, and serious climatic changes, altering weather patterns. Air pollution in the form of contaminants from aerosol cans and the burning of tropical rain forests is apparently responsible for punching a large hole in the ozone layer which protects people and animals from the damaging ultraviolet rays of the sun. As a result, skin cancer is on the rise.

The Cuyahoga River in northern Ohio has twice burst spontaneously into flame, illustrating another major problem, *water pollution*. All major rivers and lakes have been treated, intentionally or not, as dumping grounds for waste products. Inadequate sewage treatment and industrial wastes are poured into them, as well as into the oceans. Detergents not only cause streams and sewers to foam, but by adding excessive nutrients to lakes bring about a rapid growth of algae and other plant life. The algae choke the waters and make them undrinkable. Afterward the algae decompose and consume the deep water oxygen vital to fish. This process, known as eutrophication, creates "dead" lakes. Animal wastes from feed lots and oil slicks from accidents involving tankers and offshore drilling also threaten the earth's water. Millions of tons of oil are dumped annually into the oceans. What all the negative effects of this might be is not yet clearly known. One thing we do know is that it is happening at the same time as increasing numbers of people have a greater need for clean water. Are we on a collision course with the results of our own practices?

What are preachers to say about this? Two options are certainly dead ends: We can neither ignore the ecological crisis, on the assumption that science and technology will solve the problem, nor can we simply repeat traditional Christian statements about creation and providence. While the problem cannot be solved without science and technology, neither can it be solved by them alone. We must understand two things: that radical changes in lifestyles are called for and that science and technology need to become much more respectful of the earth than they have been.[19] What "radical changes in lifestyles" means is, as Cobb and Griffin argue, that "frugality and communality must replace conspicuous consumption and individualism."[20] Nor can we repeat traditional statements about creation and providence. The Christian tradition is at least partly responsible for our current ecological crisis, for the following reasons. It understood God as absolutely separate from the world, and viewed the order of the world as incapable of change "throughout the life history of creation."[21] Traditionally, the earth was primarily viewed as the "stage" on which the historical drama of redemption was enacted. The interrelatedness of human beings and nature was not understood.

What process theology can help preachers develop both in themselves and in their congregations is an ecological sensitivity and a theology for survival, one that stresses both justice and sustainability.[22] Central to this would be an understanding of the relation between God and the world—expressed in models and metaphors that are appropriate both to the Christian faith and to the age in which we live—which recognizes that because the world is God's body, what affects the world affects God. Can we come to understand that when the opulent diversity of the biosphere is diminished, God is impoverished?[23] When process theologians speak of God's "unbounded love," God's love for each and all, they include the entire realm of nature within God's care and concern. God's limitless love is unsurpassably broad and deep, including animals, "plants and inorganic realities such as mountains, rivers, stars, and wind."[24] The empathic God of process theism is a life-centered God. As Jay McDaniel argues, appropriate response to such a God would entail a life-centered spirituality.[25] Such a relational, connective, and non-dominating understanding of stewardship can be particularly well developed from the interchange between insights from process thought and biblical understandings.[26]

Process theology can also help us understand that human beings and human history are not separate from nature and natural processes but, however much we transcend nature, integrally participate in and interact with a larger environment. Indeed, we do not merely have an environment but are ourselves part of the environment of all other beings, God included. "The whole of nature participates in us and we in it."[27] As Whitehead remarked, "There is no possibility of detached, self-contained local existence. The environment enters into the nature of each thing."[28] Also—because it regards each actual individual, including the occasions which comprise rocks, as enjoying subjective immediacy, and therefore as having intrinsic value—process thought is able to suggest, as Delwin Brown argues, that we should not merely appreciate nature but also respect it.[29]

Woman Was Created for Man

We open this discussion of sexism with this paraphrase of Paul's remark in 1 Corinthians 11:9 to indicate that here, too, the Christian tradition is a part of the problem and needs to undergo revision if it is to address helpfully the systemic injustice of sexism. Paul's remarks in the above context, that man is "the image and glory of God; but woman is the glory of man" (1 Cor. 11:7, RSV), exhibit the depth of the problem. Whether Paul's comments were sexist is disputed by scholars. What is beyond argument is that the church has long taken such remarks as warranting unjust practices toward women.

The desert father Jerome (ca. 342-420) regarded marriage as evil and virginity as good, claiming that in Eden Eve was a virgin and that married life began only after the fall.[30] The only justification for marriage is that is produces virgins: "I gather the rose from the thorn."[31] Mary the virgin is contrasted with Eve as the two sources, respectively, of life and death. Priests cannot pray unless they abstain from sexual intercourse with women, and since they are to pray constantly they must be celibate.[32] Because woman, being closer to nature and less rational than man, has more difficulty in quenching her "burning lust," a wise man will not take a wife.[33]

Augustine of Hippo (ca. 354-430) took a more moderate view of these matters than Jerome, looking upon sexual union in marriage as justified by the intention to have children.[34] The sex drive, which Augustine saw as "carnal concupiscence," is tolerated within marriage because of the purpose of marriage. Obviously, birth control, to which Augustine refers as the use of the "evil appliance," is forbidden because it would thwart the only justification for married sex.[35]

Thomas Aquinas (ca. 1225-1274) summarized and systematized the tradition of the church on women and many of his views remain efficacious today. He adopted Aristotle's view that women are misbegotten males, regarding each individual woman (though not women as a gender) as "defective and misbegotten."[36] Women as such are not defective, but good, because they are necessary to human reproduction. Given her defectiveness, "woman is naturally subject to man, because in man the discretion of reason predominates."[37] Because Adam was created first, "the man is the head of the woman."[38] Woman is a help to man only in reproduction of human beings; in any other endeavor, another man would be a more effective help.[39] Nor can women be ordained because they are "in the state of subjection." Rather, "the male sex is required for receiving Orders."[40]

Views such as these are never mere theories. Theory is always related to practice and sexist theories both justify and reinforce sexist practice. Sexist practice characteristically assigns authority to males and submission to women. Of all such forms of control, says Harvey Cox, "man's domination of women is the oldest and most persistent."[41] D. H. Lawrence trenchantly remarked that man is willing to accept woman as "an angel, a devil, a baby-face, a machine, an instrument, a bosom, a womb, a pair of legs, a servant, an encyclopaedia, an ideal or an obscenity; the one thing he won't accept her as is a human being."[42]

Sexism in the Christian tradition constitutes a massive distortion of the message that Christianity offers. It "systematically denigrates woman....affirms women's inferiority and subordination to men, and excludes women from full actualization and participation in the church and society."[43] Its view of Eve as the initiator of evil projects evil on to woman as the original "other." Sexism is related to classism and racism, as is shown by the facts that the majority of the poor are women and those dependent on them (children and the elderly), and that black women in the United States face the triple jeopardy of being black and women and among the poorest of the poor.[44] What is called the "feminization of poverty" means that among those living in poverty women are dramatically increasing both in absolute numbers and percentages. Hence in spite of some gains on behalf of women's liberation, the overall situation of women remains one of being marginalized, powerless, poverty-ridden, and subject to the stresses that affect people in such conditions.

The feminist/process theologian Rita Nakashima Brock argues that the church has neither "understood the extent to which it is involved in patriarchy" nor been aware of the "abuse and pain at the heart of our society, the family, which is one of the social institutions most important to the maintenance of male dominance."[45] Christianity has been blissfully ignorant of the heartache caused to women and children at its very center.

> In the United States suicide is the second most common form of death among teenagers; one in every five children grows up in poverty; one in every three women will be raped as an adult, one in every four daughters and one in every eight sons are molested by the age of eighteen; and every thirty-nine seconds a women is battered in her own home. Homicide is the fifth leading cause of death for American children ages one through eighteen and 1.4 million children annually, ages three through seventeen, are physically abused. Adrienne Rich has called the family home the most dangerous place in America for women.[46]

Because in sexism they are theoretically less than fully human, women are discounted, invisible. They are invisible not only in the history and tradition of the church but even in discussions pertaining to women's issues. The fetus which cannot be seen is more visible in the abortion controversy than the woman who can be seen. Whatever one's view of that question, certainly the woman should not be discounted.

What those who are struggling for the liberation of women want is freedom. The constant form that freedom takes has to do with the right to be self-determining, self-directing, and self-creative. For process theology, freedom is a dipolar notion, entailing both creativity and context.[47] Heretofore in this chapter we have stressed the context(s) of freedom in the forms of various systemic injustices. Contexts determine but do not wholly determine us; we are partially determined, partially indetermined, with "room" left over for our own decisions as to how we actualize our intentions and purposes. Women seek contexts that are not unnecessarily restrictive, and greater room for their self-determination. In different contexts this will mean different things. For American middle-class women it means freedom from exploitation in the work force, equality in pay and opportunity for employment, quality child care, freedom to live one's own life and not merely to live vicariously through a husband, freedom from enforced triviality, and freedom from being reduced to an object of sexual exploitation for purposes of advertising and consumerism.

For black women in America it means liberation from the triple jeopardy of racism, classism, and sexism. Women in Third World countries might well regard freedom, concretely, quite differently, as the freedom to have sufficient food to eat, jobs for husbands, and education for children. The increasing number of women showing up among the homeless in America would regard secure shelter as liberating. What is constant about freedom is the right to be herself. But the concrete meaning of this varies accordingly as the things from which women need to be free and the things for which they hope differ from one context to another.

The church today increasingly talks of itself as the "church of the poor." This it cannot be unless it is also the "church of and for women," the poorest of the poor. For preachers to speak responsibly on behalf of the good news for women, they will have to develop new models for what it means to be human. Traditional Christian anthropology, with its hierarchical dualisms of spirit/matter and body/soul, has been "enormously destructive of women."[48] Also, new ways of "naming" God, new metaphors for expressing God's all-inclusive love, ones that are helpful to us in this age, will be needed.

Process theology can help overcome the difficulties lying at the base of sexism and enable preachers to think and talk appropriately of women. The dualisms of spirit/matter, mind/body, for example, are completely overthrown by process thought. Indeed they are prime examples of what Whitehead meant by "incoherence," because once having split body and mind from each other, dualists cannot explain their obvious relatedness. For process thought, spirit and matter, mind and body are two different ways of speaking of one complex occasion of experience. In its role of receiving the past into itself, the occasion "physically" feels what is given to it; in the role of synthesizing that past with novel possibilities to imagine alternatives, its "mental" pole comes into play. Here "physical" and "mental" refer to different kinds of feelings, both of which are important. Similarly, the human being is "dipolar," having a body which is the most intimate part of the external environment and which "houses" the self, which is that part of the body that entertains intense experience and "presides" over the whole. The self or spirit can only express itself through the body; meaning is always expressed bodily; the body is "the sensitive amplifier of the meanings of the spirit."[49]

We have already written of new ways of naming God, thinking of the world as God's body, and using female metaphors for God. Here we want to stress Whitehead's new idea of God, which was developed in opposition to the view that God acts on the world but receives nothing from it, that God is wholly self-sufficient, and that God's power is coercive. "Thus," as Cobb and Griffin contend, "Whitehead was rejecting from his metaphysical idea of God elements that are stereotypically masculine."[50] Whitehead's new idea was that the world affects God, as well as that God affects the world, that God has "physical" feelings of the world (which is God's "consequent" nature), that the world is immanent in God. In this way Whitehead stressed God's "responsive love, God's tenderness, and God's sharing of human suffering."[51] The images of God that Whitehead associated with his idea of God were those of God's patience and tenderness, of God as suffering with us, of God's redeeming of us as keeping us everlastingly secure in God's life. Consequently, process theology also calls for the creation of new language for God, language that does not demean women by implying that what is ultimately real are those characteristics associated with the traditional "strong male."

War and Rumors of War

The next systemic injustice is that of a death-loving and ever expanding militarism. Militarism is the violent use of force to defend unequal relationships. This can be done internally in a country, through a variety of forms of military and surveillance techniques, or externally through massive intelligence, espionage and military force. Since the end of World War II militarism has reached its zenith in the nuclear arms race. A 1983 study by Ruth L. Sivard showed that "1.3 million dollars *per minute* on average are spent for military purposes; during the same minute 30 children die for lack of food or simple vaccines."[52] In other words, in every hour of 1983, 78 million dollars were spent for military purposes and 1,800 children perished for lack of food and elementary vaccinations. In August 1988 Dr. James Grant, executive director of the United Nations Children's Fund, reported that more than 3.5 million children died in 1987 because they "didn't have fifty cents worth of vaccine in their veins."[53] Counting children and adults together, 50,000 a day "die prematurely from readily preventable causes."[54] That is the human cost of militarism, entirely apart from casualties in military action.

More than thirty years ago, leading thinkers began pointing out the dilemma in which we now find ourselves with regard to militarism. Preparation for war, particularly in the form of military budgets, has become a central feature of many contemporary societies.[55] It shapes "their scientific endeavor, limits their intellectual effort, swells the national budgets of the world, and has replaced what was once called diplomacy."[56] Further, the prospect of nuclear war, total war with absolute weapons, has rendered our conventional thinking about war useless. Gone are strategic targets; whole areas of the earth, perhaps the earth itself, are targeted. Gone is the distinction between military and civilian; the earth's population is under threat. Gone is the distinction between attack and defense; indeed, to attack even successfully is to lose. C. Wright Mills commented: "We are at the very end of the military road. It leads nowhere but to death. With war, all nations will fail. Yet the preparation for World War III is the most strenuous and massive effort of the leading societies of the world today. War has become total. And war has become absurd."[57]

We have also placed the ultimate decision about nuclear war increasingly in the hands of technology. Yet if the sophisticated equipment of a U.S. or U.S.S.R. radar or computer operator should suddenly develop a "glitch," we would have only about fifteen minutes for the various "fail safe" mechanisms to come into operation. History is not reassuring as to the reliability of fail-safe mechanisms and the human beings who operate them. The final war could start by accident, except that the chief conditions of the "accident" are not themselves accidental; they are deliberate. These conditions trace back to the decision to try "to solve the problems of absolute peace, presented by nuclear weapons, by concentrating...upon instruments of genocide."[58] One of the chief difficulties in changing this situation is that economic prosperity is believed by many to be grounded in the war economy. And there is at least evidence for this view, as repeated defense contract scandals indicate. There is profit to be made in preparing for war and competition, both legal and illegal, for military contracts is intense. Yet surely in this age of the total and final weapon, the only realistic military view of things is that war itself is now our biggest enemy, not the enemy against whom it should defend us.

Thirty years ago, however, thinkers opposing preparations for nuclear war hardly had in mind the kinds of consequences that such a war would bring. They were attentive for the most part only to human casualties. Today, scientists are alerting us to other and more far-reaching aspects of the nuclear aftermath, pointing to a catastrophic range of atmospheric, climatic, radiological, and biological consequences. As a result of the incredible cloud of dust and soot that would cover much of the earth, even summertime temperatures would be reduced to levels well below freezing, with most daylight cut off. This is the "nuclear winter" that is now predicted to follow the most likely kind of nuclear war.

The human casualties are drastic enough—with one billion people being killed immediately by blast, heat, and radiation and another billion dying later from the delayed effects of radioactivity and the destruction of life-support systems.[59] But this is only the beginning of the story.

The four main atmospheric effects would be "obscuring smoke in the troposphere, obscuring dust in the stratosphere, the fallout of radioactive debris, and the partial destruction of the ozone layer."[60] Fresh water would freeze for months to a depth of several feet, agriculture would be wiped out, and not even the southern hemisphere would be spared. From nuclear war there is no sanctuary. Nor in this war can an effective "first strike" of nuclear weapons be used: "If Nation A attacks Nation B with an effective first strike, counterforce only [targeting only weapons sites, not cities], then Nation A has thereby committed suicide, even if Nation B has not lifted a finger to retaliate."[61] The cold and dark twilight of midday would be a situation in which any life would have a hard time surviving; the most successful at it would probably be rats and insects. Virtually all cities would cease to be; the fabric of contemporary society, its electronic and material infrastructure, would be destroyed. The human know-how necessary to rebuild would itself be gone. Medical care would be nonexistent for any who might survive. "The fates of the 2-3 billion people who were not killed immediately—including those in nations far removed from targets—might in many ways be worse."[62]

The ecosystems on which we depend for fresh air, water, waste disposal, nutrients, soil, pest control, food, and the genetic "library" would be assaulted by darkness, cold, wildfires, toxic smog, dangerous ultraviolet radiation, nuclear radiation, acid rain, pollution of all the waters, and incredibly violent storms.[63] Photosynthesis would cease, and with it all animals, including the human ones, would perish. Paraphrasing scripture, biologist Paul Ehrlich remarks: "All flesh is truly 'grass.'"[64] The damage to the ozone layer would permit ultraviolet light to reach ground level, where it would attack the immune systems of mammals as well as lead to widespread blindness. Extensive radioactive fallout would be deadly to all exposed people and to many species of plants and animals.

Fires started by nuclear blasts could continue to burn for months or years as oil wells, coal supplies, peat marshes, and coal seams were ignited. Wildfires burning cities and forests would destroy vast areas. In World War II, Hamburg was hit by a firestorm that sent flames 15,000 feet into the air and smoke 40,000 feet high. The fire was hot enough to melt aluminum, and underground shelters were so hot that when opened "and oxygen admitted, flammable materials and even corpses burst into flames."[65] Yet one nuclear firestorm could easily be more than 100 times larger than the Hamburg firestorm.

Preachers might well feel reluctant to talk about such matters, preferring to leave them to the "experts." But the experts are the people who have gotten all of us and the earth itself into a situation where our nuclear arsenals now are the equivalent of one million

Hiroshima-type nuclear weapons. Clearly the wisdom of the experts is limited; clearly the gospel might have something helpful to say to the situation.

What that will be, however, is yet to be seen. Since 1945 we have been living in an utterly unique historical situation, one in which we as a species might extinguish ourselves—"the possibility that we humans, by ourselves, will utterly destroy not only ourselves but our species, all future generations, thus bringing the human project, through which and for which many hundreds of generations have labored, to an abrupt and final halt."[66]

The very uniqueness of this situation, for which we human beings are responsible, means that certain traditional Christian ways of speaking of God in relation to human beings and the earth are "not only outmoded; they have become misleading and dangerous in important respects, and they must be thoroughly reworked."[67] Models of God that assign to God all the power, sever God from real relatedness to the world, deny to us the freedom and power necessary to act decisively now, and focus our religious attention solely or chiefly on the world to come, must be replaced with models appropriate to the gospel and to the utterly unique situation that we have created for ourselves. New models for God bring with them new models for ethics. That, too, will be useful to preachers, since the church's three traditional stances on war—pacifism, the just war, and the crusade—are all rendered as obsolete as traditional theological models.[68]

The development of nuclear power for destructive purposes is, at least to date, the most extreme and obscene result of the assumption that genuine power is coercive and compulsive. This assumption is directly contradicted by process theology. Coercive power, the ability to intervene in a situation and override the freedom of those in it, is a kind of power available only to finite agents and has a limited usefulness. Grabbing up a child and preventing it from running into the traffic is a use of coercive power which is morally positive. Turning one's wife into an object of abuse and ridicule in order to stifle her independence is another, morally negative, use of coercive power. Believing that coercive power is what is ultimately real, the kind that God wields, sanctions the attempt to override human freedom. God, who creates creatures who in turn are partially self-creative, has a kind of power that is, by definition,

persuasive rather than coercive. Only this kind of power is genuinely creative, just as the bonds of love are the only ones that really
bind us to one another.

But if God's power is persuasive, Christians will have to face
up to their own responsibilities for the outcome of history. Whereas
the omnipotent wonder-worker of traditional theism may excuse us
from responsibility, allowing us to leave all our crises in "his" hands
to dispense with as "he" will anyway, the God of process theology,
like the covenant God of the Bible, requires the cooperation of
God's covenant partners. We have to do our share. The question put
to us by such a God was nowhere better asked than by William
James:

> Suppose that the world's author put the case to you before
> creation, saying: "I am going to make a world not certain to
> be saved, a world the perfection of which shall be condi-
> tional merely, the condition being that each several agent
> does its own 'level best.' I offer you the chance of taking
> part in such a world. Its safety, you see, is unwarranted. It
> is a real adventure, with real danger, yet it may win through.
> It is a social scheme of cooperative work genuinely to be
> done. Will you join the procession? Will you trust yourself
> and trust the other agents enough to face the risk?"[69]

Classism and Racism

We look at these two systemic injustices together because to
look at them separately gives a false picture of the nature of
oppression. That we turn to them last does *not* mean that we think
them less important than the other systemic injustices. All systemic
injustices are interrelated, part and parcel of the same mess. Money
spent on militarism does not go to help ghetto residents; black
women are the worst victims of sexism; how Western culture has
treated nature and how it has treated people whom it deems
"inferior" are clearly related.

Racism as practices against blacks in America will be the topic
and the illustration of the relation between classism and racism. The
Swedish sociologist Gunnar Myrdal long ago pointed out the
"vicious cycle" of racial prejudice and its relation to economic

discrimination: Blacks are forced by exploitation into the lowest economic status which results in their having poor housing, high crime rates, high disease rates, and little ambition. These are then taken by whites as "evidence" of racial inferiority.[70] How federal budget money is spent also illustrates the relationship between militarism and other systemic injustices. From 1960 to 1967 the United States spent $348 billion on war, $27 billion on space, and $2 billion on housing and community development.[71]

There is a direct economic relation between classism and racism. The chief recipients of the service benefits of American society are the middle and upper classes. Investment in children's education is a prime example. Wealthy school districts are able to provide much better educational opportunities to children than ghetto school districts. Meanwhile the black underclass in the ghetto receives the worst of everything: "the worst housing, the worst and most ineffectual schools, the worst jobs. The only thing they receive a disproportionately high share of is unemployment and disease."[72]

It has become customary to distinguish between individual and institutional racism. Individual racism consists of overt acts and personal attitudes. The slaying of civil rights workers in Mississippi by members of the Ku Klux Klan is an instance of individual racism. Institutionally racist was the failure of the state government to bring the murderers to justice. The slavery system was a case of institutional racism, as were the Jim Crow laws. Individual racism need not express itself in institutional form and an institution may be racist although its members are comparatively free of individual racism. Reinhold Niebuhr taught us that a group can be much more sinful than its members would find tolerable in themselves.[73]

How is institutional racism reflected in American life? First, in economic structures and processes. Blacks are largely excluded from the free enterprise system. Were they to own businesses in proportion to their representation in the population, there would be ten times more black-owned companies than there are.[74] Inferior educational preparation limits the ability of blacks to conduct private enterprise; lack of adequate credit increases the difficulties blacks face in the business world. Insurance costs in inner-city ghettoes are higher than elsewhere and the increasing dominance of the economy by fewer and fewer large corporations further disadvantages blacks. Black workers are unemployed and underemployed. Compared to white families, black median family income still declines. The development of our high-technology economy reduces the number of low-skilled entry-level jobs available to blacks, while the educational system does not enable them to enter the economy at a higher level. Industry moves increasingly to the suburbs, away from most black workers, while labor unions, particularly the craft unions, remain inadequately open to black members. Meanwhile prices for black consumers in the inner city are higher than elsewhere.[75] Classism and racism obviously reinforce each other.

In 1983 blacks constituted 12 percent of the American population but had 7.2 percent of total U.S. income and controlled only 2.3 percent of its total wealth.[76] Black business firms had 0.18 percent of the total of business receipts in 1980; 4.3 percent of officials and managers of businesses in 1982 were black, while blacks held 21.8 percent of the service jobs. Of all adults with income in 1982, the median incomes of white males was $15,401, while black females' median income was $5,543. In 1983 35.7 percent of black women were living in poverty, compared to 12.1 percent of white women.[77] In 1982 2.9 percent of all lawyers and judges were black, while 47.2 percent of all household cleaners were black. The death rate of children in 1980 per 100,000 for white children under the age of 1 year was 963, but 2,124 for black children.

The "dollar gap" between the median incomes for black and white families in 1964 was $3,134; by 1984 it had become $12,254.[78] The poverty gap had not improved since Lyndon Johnson initiated the war on poverty in 1964. Whereas in 1959 25 percent of the nation's poor were black, in 1984 this had increased to 28 percent. Black median family income is not projected to equal that of white families until the year 2420,[79] a pace of development that gives a new meaning to the term "gradualism."

Institutional racism is reflected, second, in the under-education of black children. A 1966 report by the U.S. Department of Health, Education, and Welfare stated that: "In the metropolitan Northeast Negro students on the average begin the first grade with somewhat lower scores on standard achievement tests than whites, are about 1.6 grades behind white students by the sixth grade, and have fallen 3.3 grades behind white students by the twelfth grade."[80] Black young people are either in segregated schools, still, or in integrated schools which are internally segregated, largely along racial lines, into ability groups. Being placed into a lower-level ability group does nothing to enhance the self-esteem of black students. Coping with the double stigma of racism and poverty, low self-esteem is probably the biggest problem facing black students. Nor does treating black children as "slow" enhance their educational progress. As schools fail to retain the interest of students, the drop-out rate climbs along with that of teenage pregnancy.

Third, institutional racism exists in the administration of justice. Police forces are overwhelmingly white in composition and concentrate much of their attention upon black communities. Similarly, prosecutors' offices, courts, and prisons are staffed predominantly by whites, except for the janitorial services. A very small proportion of lawyers are black, which means that black defendants have difficulty securing representation that can be said to understand the person being defended. "In the typical case, the black person suspected of a crime is arrested by a white police officer, brought to face a white judge, district attorney, and jury in a courtroom where the proceedings are recorded by white clerks, and upon conviction sent to a prison where the only black employees are custodians."[81] Class bias is introduced into the justice system by the inability of many black defendants to pay the costs of bail. Consequently, they spend time before trial in jail and appear in court in prison dress. Statistically, people showing up in court in jailhouse fatigues are more often found guilty than defendants who are able to make bail and who appear in court dressed in middle-class style.[82] Justice is like any other commodity: You get what you pay for. The inability of blacks to pay means that they get less justice.

Other forms of institutional racism also exist in America. A complete review would deal with such matters as the failure of political parties to accord full participation to blacks and of the health-care delivery system to provide adequate services to blacks. Our purpose here, however, is not to describe what is set forth more adequately in hundreds of places, but to bring the question of racism and classism to the attention of those who would preach the Christian faith in a way appropriate to the gospel and adequate to the realities of our contemporary life. Surely if the gospel is not only the promise of the love of God freely offered to each and all but also and for that very reason the command of God that justice be done to each and all, the pulpit cannot remain silent on racism and classism.

Process theology has no magic wand to wave that will resolve the problem of racism in America. Many theologies and theological ethics can be helpful to preachers on this topic, as indeed can the fundamental witness of the Bible, if they will but be employed. The contribution process thought can make is to call into question the individualism or privatism that is so much at the heart of both American religion and American racism. Just as American religion has been largely privatized, so do many people think that the very purpose of society, government, and public life is to serve and defend private life. Douglas Sturm's communitarian ethics based on process thought argues against the thesis that "civil society is subordinate to the happiness of the individual."[83] The reason why so many middle and upper-middle class people in our society and churches are indifferent to such fundamental issues as racism and classism is that, from their point of view, the political-economic process is working rather well; they're happy. In Australia this is the "I'm all right, Jack" attitude. Indeed, as the economic analysis of racism and classism summarized here shows, they benefit economically from racism. The qualification of this latter point is that some observers are learning that an undereducated underclass does not help American industry compete with Japan and that this is a national problem, not merely a problem for those immediately victimized by it.

As against the individualism that lies behind racism and classism, process theology stresses our internal relatedness to all others and God's internal relatedness to all others. Racism and individualism ultimately impoverish both us and God; owning our essential relatedness would enable us "to claim the community as integral to ourselves, necessary for ourselves."[84] We must discover our solidarity with the oppressed. Will the church be a teacher in this regard?

Notes

[1]See James A. Sanders' criticism of lectionaries in his "Canon and Calendar: An Alternative Lectionary Proposal," in *Social Themes of the Christian Year*, ed. Dieter T. Hessel (Philadelphia: The Geneva Press, 1983), pp. 257-263.

[2]Rodney Stark, *et al.*, *Wayward Shepherds*, p. 90.

[3]*Ibid.*, p. 91.

[4]*Ibid.*, p. 92.

[5]James L. Guth and Helen Lee Turner, "Pastoral Politics in the 1988 Election: Disciples as Compared to Presbyterians and Southern Baptists," in *A Case Study of Mainstream Protestantism: The Disciples' Relation to American Culture, 1880-1989*, ed. D. Newell Williams (Grand Rapids: Eerdmans, and St. Louis: Chalice Press,1991).

[6]Joseph E. Faulkner, "What Are They Saying?," in *ibid.*

[7]Stark, *Wayward Shepherds*, p. 95.

[8]*Ibid.*

[9]*Ibid.*, p. 102

[10]John B. Cobb, Jr., *Process Theology as Political Theology* (Philadelphia: Westminster, 1982), p. 48.

[11]*Ibid.*, p. 51.

[12]See, e.g., James A. Sanders, *Canon and Community* (Philadelphia: Fortress Press, 1984). The compatibility between Sanders' understanding of the norm of appropriateness and that of Schubert M. Ogden was pointed out by Clark Williamson, "The Authority of Scripture After the *Shoah*," in *Faith and Creativity*, ed. George Nordgulen and George W. Shields (St. Louis: CBP Press, 1987), p. 141. The difference between Sanders and Ogden on this point is that Sanders finds the norm operating in scripture where Israel's hermeneutical axioms are brought into play, whereas Ogden wants to locate the norm *behind* scripture in the "earliest apostolic witness" to Jesus Christ.

[13]McFague, *Models of God*, chap. 1.

[14]*The Indianapolis Star*, June 12, 1988.

[15]*Ibid.*

[16]John W. Klotz, *Ecology Crisis: God's Creation and Man's Pollution* (St. Louis: Concordia, 1971), p. 5.

[17]*Ibid.*, p. 50.

[18]*Ibid.*, p. 60.

[19]See particularly the essays in David R. Griffin, ed., *The Reenchantment of Science* (Albany: SUNY Press, 1988).

[20]John B. Cobb, Jr., and David R. Griffin, *Process Theology: An Introductory Exposition*, p. 150.

[21]Julian N. Hartt, "Creation and Providence," in *Christian Theology: An Introduction to Its Traditions and Tasks*, ed. Hodgson and King, p. 145.

[22]See Charles Birch and John B. Cobb, Jr., *The Liberation of Life*.

[23]Cobb and Griffin, *Process Theology*, p. 151.

[24]Jay McDaniel, *Of God and Pelicans* (Louisville: Westminster/John Knox Press, 1989), p. 21.

[25]*Ibid.*, pp. 85-110.

[26]Clark Williamson, "Good Stewards of God's Varied Grace," *Encounter*, Vol. 47 (Winter 1986), pp. 61-83.

[27]Cobb and Griffin, *Process Theology*, p. 155.

[28]Alfred North Whitehead, *Modes of Thought* (New York: Macmillan, 1938), p. 188.

[29]Delwin Brown, "'Respect for the Rocks:' Toward a Christian Process Theology of Nature," *Encounter*, Vol. 50 (Autumn 1989), p. 318.

[30]Jerome, "Letter to Eustochium" in *Women and Religion*, ed. Elizabeth Clark and Herbert Richardson (New York: Harper & Row, 1977), p. 59.

[31]*Ibid.*, p. 60.

[32]*Ibid.*, p. 63.

[33]*Ibid.*, p. 66.

[34]Augustine, "On Marriage and Concupiscence," in *Women and Religion*, ed. Elizabeth Clark and Herbert Richardson (New York: Harper & Row, 1977), p. 72.

[35]*Ibid.*, p. 75.

[36]Thomas Aquinas, "On the Production of Woman," in *Women and Religion*, ed. Elizabeth Clark and Herbert Richardson (New York: Harper & Row, 1977), p. 87.

[37]*Ibid.*, p. 88.

[38]*Ibid.*

[39]*Ibid.*, p. 92.

[40]*Ibid.*, p. 96.

[41]Cited in Letty Russell, *Human Liberation in a Feminist Perspective—A Theology*, p. 145.

[42]Cited in *ibid.*, p. 148.

[43]Anne E. Carr, *Transforming Grace: Christian Tradition and Women's Experience* (San Francisco: Harper & Row, 1988), p. 95.

[44]*Ibid.*, p. 103.

[45]Rita Nakashima Brock, *Journeys by Heart* (New York: Crossroad, 1988), p. 2f.

[46]*Ibid.*, p. 3.

[47]See Delwin Brown, *To Set at Liberty* (Maryknoll: Orbis Books, 1981), pp. 31, 33-36.

[48]David H. Kelsey, "Human Being," in *Christian Theology: An Introduction to Its Traditions and Tasks*, p. 173.

[49]On the topic of the unity of body and mind (or spirit), Whitehead's discussions in *Modes of Thought*, pp. 21-32, 114-115, are especially helpful.

[50]Cobb and Griffin, *Process Theology*, p. 133.

[51]*Ibid.*

[52]Matthew L. Lamb, "Liberation Theology and Social Justice," *Process Studies*, Vol. 14 (1985), p. 103.

[53]*Manchester Guardian Weekly*, Vol. 139, No. 7, August 14, 1988, p. 6.
[54]*Ibid.*
[55]C. Wright Mills, *The Causes of World War Three* (New York: Simon and Schuster, 1958), p. 1.
[56]*Ibid.*, p. 2.
[57]*Ibid.*, p. 4.
[58]Lewis Mumford, cited in *ibid.*, p. 48.
[59]Paul R. Ehrlich, Carl Sagan *et al.*, *The Cold and the Dark* (New York: W. W. Norton & Co., 1984), p. xxiii.
[60]*Ibid.*, p. 11.
[61]*Ibid.*, p. 33.
[62]*Ibid.*, p. 45.
[63]*Ibid.*, p. 46f.
[64] bid., p. 48.
[65]*Ibid.*, p. 53.
[66]Gordon Kaufman, *Theology for a Nuclear Age* (Philadelphia: Westminster Press, 1985), p. 5.
[67]*Ibid.*, p. 9.
[68]Ronald E. Osborn, ed., *Seeking God's Peace in a Nuclear Age* (St. Louis: CBP Press, 1985), p. 22.
[69]William James, *Pragmatism* (Cleveland: The World Publishing Co., 1955), p. 187.
[70]Gunnar Myrdal, *An American Dilemma* (New York: Harper & Row, 1964), p. 75ff.
[71]Louis L. Knowles and Kenneth Prewitt, eds., *Institutional Racism in America* (Englewood Cliffs, NJ: Prentice-Hall, Inc., 1969), p. 119.
[72]Harold M. Baron, "The Web of Urban Racism," in *ibid.*, p. 165.
[73]Reinhold Niebuhr, *Moral Man and Immoral Society* (New York: Charles Scribner's Books, 1932), pp. xi-xii.
[74]Knowles and Prewitt, *Institutional Racism in America*, p. 16.
[75]*Ibid.*, pp. 25-29.
[76]*Fact Sheets on Institutional Racism* (New York: Council on Interracial Books for Children, 1984), p. 2.
[77]*Ibid.*, p. 7.
[78]Theodore Cross, *The Black Power Imperative* (New York: Faulkner Books, 1984), p. 208.
[79]*Ibid.*, p. 206.
[80]"Equality of Educational Opportunity" (U.S. Department of Health, Education, and Welfare: 1966), p. 20.
[81]Knowles and Prewitt, *Institutional Racism*, p. 66.
[82]*Ibid.*, p. 73.
[83]Douglas Sturm, *Community and Alienation* (Notre Dame: University of

Notre Dame Press, 1988), p. 1.

[84]*Ibid.*, p. 2.

Chapter

Process Hermeneutics

In this chapter we deal with the question of how a process theological approach to preaching would go about the task of interpreting biblical texts. Much has been written on the topic of process hermeneutics, i.e., how process thinkers interpret the process of interpretation, and we do not intend to go over that ground here.[1] What we will do is to lay out our approach to process hermeneutics in terms of its (somewhat) distinctive features and with regard to some of the central categories and insights of process thought. Also we will give a few examples of how process hermeneutics works. Subsequently, we will turn our attention to the question of how preachers might deal with biblical texts and provide a method for doing so.

A Norm of Appropriateness

First, we begin with the question of a norm of appropriateness for guiding the interpretation of biblical texts. We start here because the lack of such a norm is a perceived weakness in process hermeneutics generally. Process hermeneutics is aware of the

developmental nature of meaning and takes an inclusive approach
to allowing the various and sometimes conflicting motifs in scripture to come to expression. This very strength of process
hermeneutics, as Barry Woodbridge has seen, "points to the need
for some form of normative assistance."[2] Woodbridge himself
seeks this normative assistance in "the social context of interpretation and the possibility of the self-transcendence of this
hermeneutic."[3] The social context of interpretation includes both
the larger guild of biblical scholarship with which any responsible
interpreter must be in conversation as well as the "entire community" of the church. Certainly Woodbridge is correct in noting that
a large and diverse community of interpreters would provide a
corrective to interpretation. He is also on target in remarking upon
the self-transcending character of process hermeneutics, which, by
virtue of its emphasis that interpretation is always in process,
recognizes that no particular interpretation is ever the last word on
the subject. Yet we are reluctant to let the matter rest here because
neither communal discourse nor failure to have the last word
guarantees that a criterion of appropriateness will be brought to bear
on the results of interpretation. We are aware, for example, that the
community of interpretation in Nazi Germany tended to support an
anti-Jewish reading of scripture, and that the larger community of
the church had been long conditioned by the "teaching of contempt"
for Jews and Judaism to lend its support to or acquiesce in that same
interpretation.

One insight shared by process thought with other interpreters of
scripture, regarding the difficulty of arriving at a norm of appropriateness, stresses that scripture itself is the result of, is embedded in,
and results in a long historical process of interpretation and
reinterpretation. "Tradition," as process thinkers use the term, is
very close to its Latin root, *traditio*, meaning "to hand on." But this
"handing on" is no static procedure by which we merely pass on,
unrevised, what we earlier received. No process thinker has better
seen the critical/constructive character of tradition than Schubert
M. Ogden:

> ...no religious tradition can long continue as a vital source
> of faith and life unless it is critically appropriated in each
> new historical situation. The importance of such tradition

always lies in the precious freight of meaning it bears, not in the forms of expression through which that meaning is borne from the past to the present. All such forms are only more or less adequate to the actual occurrence of tradition, and they are to be retained, if at all, only because or insofar as they still make possible the "handing over" which the word "tradition" (*traditio*) originally signifies. Since whether any given forms of expression continue to serve this purpose is determined by our ever-changing historical situations, the more radical the changes from one situation to another, the more urgent and far-reaching the task of a critical interpretation of the tradition.[4]

Although Ogden's remarks are made in the service of defining the contemporary theological task, they also describe how the biblical and post-biblical traditions themselves developed. The Bible itself, as James Barr argues, "is the product of a long process of formation and revision of *traditions*." The Bible as we have it— what is known as the "canon"—is the "final precipitate from this long fluid state of tradition."[5] Before there were "scriptures" in the sense of "writings," there were traditions, both oral and written, and before there was a "Bible" there were books. The canon was "late," being formally established in the Western church only around the year 400. But establishment of the canon did not so much put an end to the critical/creative development of church tradition as it changed its character, enabling other pre-canonical tradition to disappear from view and rendering the post-canonical tradition exegetical.[6]

Barr's conclusion coheres nicely with a process perspective on the same subject. He would revise the traditional model "God— revelation—scripture—church" to "God—people—tradition— scripture," with revelation "deriving from all stages alike" rather than being simply located in the past.[7] In light of his own remarks, however, his model should probably be revised to read: "God— people—tradition—scripture—post-scriptural tradition," with the latter understood to extend into the present and future, and with, as he says, revelation "deriving from all stages alike." Part and parcel of Barr's approach involves recognizing that the standard way in which we approach scripture has for too long been "dominated by *the past,"* whereas the "functioning of the Bible is much more directed towards *the future.*"[8] At this point, a process hermeneutics would agree with Barr's emphasis, convinced as it is that "what the text might come to mean can theoretically be more important than anything the text has meant in the past."[9] On one level, the Bible tells the story of the past; on a deeper level it speaks of and for the future. Stories are never told of Abraham, of the prophets, and of Jesus simply to relay information about past events, but to describe the life of faith today, to indicate how God's word intersects contemporary events, or to re-present the voice of the living Christ to a community of contemporary reader/hearers. (For centuries the Bible was read aloud, not silently to oneself; indeed, silent reading developed slowly.)[10]

Now, we have seen some (but hardly all) of the characteristic themes of process hermeneutics; yet we are even more firmly convinced, amidst all this interpretation and re-interpretation for new situations, of the need for a norm of appropriateness lest interpretation go badly awry. Fortunately we find one in what James A. Sanders calls "canonical criticism," in which he focuses on what he calls the "canonical process":

> The model canonical criticism sponsors as more nearly true to what happened, and what happens, is that of the Holy Spirit at work all along the path of the canonical process: from original speaker, through what was understood by hearers; to what disciples believed was said; to how later editors reshaped the record, oral or written, of what was said; on down to modern hearings and understandings of the texts in current believing communities.[11]

This canonical process was and is one in which the believing community "contemporized earlier value-traditions to their own situation."[12] The whole of the canon is just such "adaptable wisdom," contemporized (re-interpreted) for different situations because in each situation people needed "to know ever anew *who they were and what they should do,*" amid the changes of history, culture, and fortune.[13] This "process" of contemporization "was there from the start and continues unabated through and after the periods of intense canonical process of stabilization."[14] Phyllis Trible's comment, "All scripture is a pilgrim wandering through history, engaging in new settings and ever refusing to be locked in the box of the past,"[15] nicely captures the sense of scripture and its subsequent interpretation as an adventure, a sense shared by process thinkers.

What distinguishes Sanders' views of canonical process is that he finds a hermeneutic running through the biblical authors and editors, a hermeneutic that is the Bible's "self-corrective apparatus."[16] This self-corrective, self-critical hermeneutic guided the critical and new interpretations generated by the biblical communities over five different cultural eras of tumultuous change, from the bronze age to the Roman era. The conspicuous features of the Bible's self-correcting hermeneutic are: (1) It is a monotheizing literature (as Israel was influenced by and borrowed from her neighbors, Israel struggled to monotheize what was borrowed, affirming God's oneness); (2) Israel used a "broad theocentric hermeneutic," in which there were two axioms, (a) the *constitutive* axiom that bespeaks God's love for Israel or the church and (b) the *prophetic* axiom that manifests God's love for *all* God's people (and creatures). The constitutive axiom was brought into play when the community was in distress and needed to be reminded of God's special (but not exclusive) love for it, the prophetic when the community thought God loved it exclusively and needed to be reminded of God's love for each and all, as well as of God's command that justice be done to each and all. The constitutive axiom gives voice to God's singular love, graciously offered, the prophetic to God's singular command, understood as calling for the proper response to God's grace. (3) "*God betrays a divine bias for the weak and dispossessed.*"[17] This is a pervasive if not omnipresent axiom of biblical hermeneutics, and is a necessary articulation of the prophetic axiom lest the latter be rendered abstract to economically and socially privileged readers.

Sanders enables us to affirm both the processive, developmental nature of biblical tradition without falling into the relativism in which such an affirmation might normally result. We can formulate his various axioms of canonical hermeneutics more crisply by claiming, as we do, that the good news that runs throughout scripture is the promise of the love of God graciously offered to each and all and the command of God that we love God, in return, with all our selves and our neighbors as ourselves. Love for the neighbor implies and requires justice to the neighbor, lest love become the formal and empty sentimentality to which it has so often degenerated in Christian history. So the gospel is an ellipse with two foci, the grace and command, gift and claim of God, neither of which may be forgotten.

This formulation, the theocentrically understood gospel of the promise of God lovingly offered to each and all and the command of God that justice be done to each and all, we shall take as our norm of appropriateness for guiding interpretation.

Application of the Norm

At this point, however, we need to be cautious not to rush to judgment about particular passages, hastily labeling them "inappropriate" because they seem to violate the norm. There are in Paul, for example, several passages that clearly articulate the view that we are judged by our works. In dealing with the, shall we say, "interesting sins" committed by some within the church at Corinth, Paul argued that transgression would bring suffering and death (1 Cor. 11:27–34), that punishment and exclusion could be meted out by the community, particularly for those who commit incest *[porneia]* (1 Cor. 5:5, 9–13), that reward and punishment would be meted out at the judgment (1 Cor. 3:5—4:6), and that Christians can lose their status for committing the sins of idolatry or sexual immorality (1 Cor. 6:9–10).

One could read all such passages (regardless of whether we have, here, correctly understood them) as simply "works-righteous," and dismiss them as inappropriate or one could read them works-righteously and use them to affirm a "reward and punishment" understanding of the gospel. What we need to do, instead, is to remember a few things. First, neither Paul nor other biblical writers presented their thought as systematicians, always carefully balancing all the proper themes in one coherent statement. They often wrote as homileticians or rhetoricians, saying whatever needed to be said to make the point. Because Paul's gospel affirmed both the singular grace and the singular command of God, it is not difficult to see that sometimes we find the one emphasis in some passages, the other in others. Paul does think, as E. P. Sanders says, "that Christians should behave correctly, and one of the words that he uses to indicate that behavior is 'law': they should fulfill the law."[18] Indeed, the whole law is summarized in the command to love the neighbor (Gal. 5:14), and Paul, the Pharisee, never forgot what was included in the summary. In the language common to process thought, God is the gracious and primordial ground of our being and becoming, the one who calls us forward to a new and transformed life; God does not require us to become anything the possibility of which God does not graciously give to us. Yet God does have an aim in view for us, and missing it is sin. The inverse procedure would apply to any passage that articulated a view of grace devoid of any command on God's part. By itself, grace that requires nothing by way of response is not worth getting excited about, is "cheap grace." Any such passage, should we find one, would have to be held in tension with the other pole of the gospel.

Concern with Credibility

As process thinkers see things, we need to be concerned not only with appropriateness but with moral and intellectual credibility as well.[19] Actually, these three criteria—appropriateness, credibility, and moral plausibility—are by no means separate from one another. We might do better to speak of one complex criterion with three relatively distinct aspects. The gospel of the promise of God's love freely offered to each and all and the command of God that justice be done to each and all is not only the norm of appropriateness, but clearly contains a strong moral component. So to say that an interpretation of scripture must be morally credible simply highlights part of what is involved in saying that it must be appropriate to the gospel.

What is less clearly seen is that the gospel also requires us to make sense. Process thinkers are sometimes accused of importing into scripture an alien concern for sense making. Process thinkers, of course, do not find themselves guilty of this charge. What we see is that within the process of reinterpretation going on in scripture itself, sense making is a central concern. Indeed, one reason why Israel and the church reinterpreted their traditions from age to age and generation to generation was to "make sense" of the new situations in which they found themselves in the light of their traditions and to "make sense" of their traditions in the light of their new situations. To accomplish this double task, they had to interpret the new situation in the light of the tradition, but they had to reinterpret the tradition in light of the new situation in order to accomplish the first task. Luke-Acts, for instance, clearly seeks to come to terms with the delay of the *parousia* as well as with the enduring power of the Roman Empire and reinterprets the apocalyptic thrust of the Christian tradition accordingly.

One place where we can clearly see, in a microcosm, this kind of interpretation going on is in Matthew 7:7–11 and Luke 11:9–13.[20] This passage, from the sayings-source *Q*, is about prayer. It *promises* that if we ask, it *will* be given us; if we seek, we *will* find; if we knock, it *will* be opened to us. Reasoning from the lesser to the greater, it argues: "If you then, who are evil, know how to give good gifts to your children, how much more will your Father in heaven give *good things* to those who ask him!" (Matt. 7:11) We emphasize the words *good things* because in the Lukan version these are virtually the only words that are changed from Matthew. In Luke the closing question reads: "If you then, who are evil, know how to give good gifts to your children, how much more will the heavenly Father give *the Holy Spirit* to those who ask him!" (Luke 11:13)

At this point, Luke, which was probably written later, differs from Matthew. Why would Luke make such a change? For the reason that if the content of the promise "Ask, and it will be given you" is "good things," Luke was probably aware that many people prayed to God for all sorts of good things and did not receive them. Indeed, we know the same. Many pious Jews and devout Catholics died in Auschwitz, praying for a deliverance that did not come. Many African slaves died in slavery praying for a liberation that came too late. Many a family in every congregation has prayed for the life of a child, and regarded the prayer as "unanswered." Or, perhaps, they thought God said "no." Luke saw that if the promise of prayer was that God would give us all the "good things" for which we ask, then the promise looks to be false. It is not true. But Luke takes responsibility for the truth claims of the Christian faith and revises his understanding of the promise: It *is* true that if you ask, you will be given, that everyone who seeks finds. Yet, what we should ask for is not "good things" but "the Holy Spirit." If we understand how to pray as we ought, we will not ask God to give to us or provide for us and each other the sorts of things that we are responsible for providing for each other. We will ask God for the one thing that God and God alone can give us, God's own personal presence to our spirits, the companionship of God's Holy Spirit. If we understand prayer appropriately, we know that its promise cannot but be true. The process of reinterpretation internal to scripture is concerned with intelligibility for the sake of appropriateness, for the sake of the promise and command of the gospel. Process thinkers hold that the concern for credibility does not stop with the close of the canon but that, as with appropriateness and moral plausibility, we must constantly subject new interpretations of the Christian tradition to critical review.

The people of the Bible "needed to know ever anew," said Sanders, "who they were and what they should do." We need ever anew to know the same things: Who are we and what should we do? What Whitehead called "rational religion" and what H. Richard Niebuhr, paraphrasing Whitehead, called "revelation," seek to answer the same questions. In Whitehead's case, rational religion seeks to make possible "a coherent ordering of life...both in respect of the elucidation of thought and in respect to the direction of conduct towards a unified purpose commanding ethical approval."[21] After quoting Whitehead's definition of rational religion, H. Richard Niebuhr speaks of revelation as "that special occasion" from which "we also derive the concepts that make possible the elucidation of all the events in our history. Revelation means this intelligible event which makes all other events intelligible...; revelation means the point at which we can begin to think and act as members of an intelligible and intelligent world of persons."[22]

Avoiding Unnecessary Abstractness

Process hermeneutics tries to avoid committing what Whitehead called the "fallacy of misplaced concreteness," mistaking the abstract for the concrete.[23] One way to commit this fallacy in hermeneutics is to forget that written language is highly abstract. Written language is that of "sight," says Whitehead, speech that of "sound."[24] "Sight" and "sound," respectively, call to mind Whitehead's distinction between perception in the mode of presentational immediacy, where sight dominates, and perception in the mode of causal efficacy. The former is clear, but does not disclose relations. The latter is vague and massive, but rich with felt relations. Written language is quite recent. Whereas "speech is as old as human nature itself," the history of writing as a practical means of reflection "may be given about five or six thousand years at the most."[25] Writing "is important, modern, and artificial."[26] Paul J. Achtemeier has emphasized that the culture of late Western antiquity, well into the early medieval period, was one of "high residual orality, which nevertheless communicated significantly by means of literary creations."[27] He points this out because modern scholars have been led "to overlook almost entirely how such an oral overlay would affect the way communication was carried on by means of written media."[28]

For our purposes, we must remember not only that a preference for oral over written traditions long persisted in the church (cf. Papias), but that for the first several hundred years of church history the general and possibly exclusive practice was to read aloud.[29] Writings were written to be read aloud, were received orally and read aloud, and the "actual writing must have been accompanied by an oral performance of the words *as they were being written down*."[30] That most writing, as in the case of Paul's letters, was dictated to a scribe only underlines this point. To read *was* to read aloud; Philip "heard" the Ethiopian reading from Isaiah (Acts 8:30). As late as the fourth century, the fact that Ambrose of Milan could read silently generated conjecture and remarks. "Reading was therefore oral performance *whenever* it occurred and in whatever circumstances. Late antiquity knew nothing of the 'silent, solitary reader.'"[31]

Whitehead reminds us that the abstraction involved in the development of language as writing "has its dangers."[32] Although important to the rise of later civilization, it can result in triviality. What this has to do with hermeneutics is fairly straightforward. Augustine, in his comments on biblical interpretation, reminded his students that in order to understand a biblical text one must decide how to "pronounce" it.[33] This emphasis has returned recently in what one process thinker calls "tone of voice" exegesis.[34]

We can see how "tone of voice" exegesis works by looking at the story of Jesus' healing of the centurion's servant (Matt. 8:5–13/ Luke 7:1–10). The centurion tells Jesus that he need not come to his house to do the healing: "Only speak the word, and my servant will be healed." The reason the centurion gives is that "I also am a man under authority, with soldiers under me; and I say to one, 'Go,' and he goes, and to another, 'Come,' and he comes, and to my slave, 'Do this,' and he does it." Jesus "marveled" at the centurion's remarks and said, "in no one in Israel have I found such faith" (Matt. 8:8–10). The story is essentially the same in Matthew and Luke, except that Matthew adds to the end of his story an anti-Jewish bite according to which "the heirs of the kingdom will be thrown into the outer darkness," while those who come from east and west will "eat with Abraham and Isaac and Jacob in the kingdom" (Matt. 8:11–12).

If we can drop Matthew's additional interpretation from our minds and think about how to *pronounce* the story, how to emphasize it in reading it aloud, how would we inflect it? Where would the stress fall in the line: "Not even in Israel have I found such faith"? If the story goes back to Jesus or to an earlier layer of the tradition, is Jesus saying—or does it have him say—that he found no trust in God's healing power in all of Israel, or is he saying that in all of Israel he never found a Jew who thought God was a general? Would he not have found in Israel "instead a God who is described by Isaiah as enfolding Israel in her arms, as holding Israel up that it might walk, sustaining Israel that it might not be faint or weary?"[35] There are two theological and scriptural reasons for asking this question. One is that if healing (salvation) is dependent on having the right kind of faith, the text proclaims a works-righteous understanding of salvation. Another is that we are given reason, elsewhere, to believe that Jesus *rejected* precisely the understanding of things that this text puts in the mouth of the centurion: "You know that among the Gentiles those whom they recognize as their rulers lord it over them, and their great ones are tyrants over them. But it is not so among you; but whoever wishes to become great among you must be your servant, and whoever wishes to be first among you must be slave of all" (Mark 10:42–44; cf. Matt. 20:26–27, Luke 20:26). The usual interpretation of the healing of the centurion's servant is both works-righteous and anti-Jewish. It buys "into a military model of the nature of God, a model full of threat and coercion, and…read[s] out scriptures in a way so wooden that it does us and them no honor."[36] A process interpretation, which stresses the relational, empathetic and persuasive nature of power, would interpret the story as the gracious gift of healing (salvation) to the servant *in spite of* the centurion's clearly patriarchal understanding of power.

Locating Jesus in Context

This discussion leads naturally into the next feature of process hermeneutics. Because it rejects the fallacy of misplaced concreteness and affirms the socio-temporal relationality of all things actual, process thought turns a critical eye upon all attempts to understand the historical Jesus by way of isolating him from his context, which inevitably in this case means his Jewish context. Everything in the real, internal constitution of any moment of experience is a grasping (prehension) of some previous occasion in the causal past of the percipient occasion. Each occasion in the life of a human being, and so each human being, is not just accidentally and externally, but internally and really, related to events in her or his environment.

To understand Jesus, therefore, we must set him in—not against—his circumambient environment in first-century Judaism, particularly that of Galilee.[37] The famous "criterion of dissimilarity," which new-questers of the historical Jesus long used to decide which teachings in the gospels could be considered as actually having come from Jesus, methodologically ruled out, in principle, all sayings that Jesus had in common with the Judaisms of his time or before. By the same token it disallowed all sayings that could be considered to reflect the interests and needs of the later church that collected the sayings.[38] The problem with using the criterion of dissimilarity to reconstruct the historical Jesus is that, as a result of it, "he becomes the embodiment of abstract principles that belong to neither history nor culture."[39] By overcoming the anti-Jewish abstractness of the historical Jesus methodologically alienated from what Bernard E. Meland calls his "communal ground of being," a process hermeneutic goes far toward overcoming the grounds for the "teaching of contempt" for Jews and Judaism that often comes to expression in commentary on Jesus of Nazareth.[40]

Interesting Propositions

Whitehead's theory of propositions holds, as do most such theories, that "a proposition must be true or false."[41] Nonetheless, being true or false is only one of the jobs of a proposition. More basically, propositions "are the tales that perhaps might be told about particular actualities."[42] As such, "its own truth, or its own falsity, is no business of a proposition."[43] Truth is the business of complex comparative feelings, or judgments, which compare propositions with the logical subjects of those propositions, in order to "test" propositions. In itself, a proposition is a "lure for feeling," a fact that makes even false propositions important: "In the real world it is more important that a proposition be interesting than that it be true. The importance of truth is that it adds to interest."[44]

Process hermeneutics employs Whitehead's understanding of the role of propositions to interpret biblical texts, regarding these texts either as housing propositions or as being, themselves, complex propositions. As such, biblical texts function as proposals for ways of understanding features of "objective reality, as important for the reader's 'forms of subjectivity.'"[45] That is to say, the text, altogether apart from whether in this or that respect its propositions are true, can nonetheless be interesting as inviting the reader/hearer to understand herself differently in relation to whatever feature of objective reality the text sets forth as important. The text may purport to describe historical events, the significance of Jesus, a miracle, the power of God, the patience of God, the importance or relative unimportance of being a member of the community (as in "I have other sheep that do not belong to this fold" [John 10:16]).

While we cannot be indifferent to questions of truth, there are times when it is more important that a scriptural proposition be interesting than that it be true. David J. Lull offers as an example the way the book of Acts depicts Paul "as one who remains a faithful observer of the law of Moses from the Damascus road to Rome, even to the point of seeing to the circumcision of the half-Gentile Timothy (16:1–3) and the observance of the Nazirite rites (21:17–26). These texts propose that the reader think of Paul, precisely in his capacity as the Christian evangelist to Gentiles *par excellence*, as at the same time the exemplary Pharisaic Jew." Whether this picture of the "historical Paul" is true, as Lull says, "has defied solution." Nonetheless, it is highly interesting; the considerations it arouses with regard to Christianity's continuity with Judaism have an "importance independent of the truth of the proposal." What is going on in the text, or between the text and the reader, is that Luke's "*proposed* picture of Paul...serves to invite approval of the author's conviction that continuity between Christianity and Israel's Scriptural religion is germane to the church's identity and self-creation."[46] This latter, a matter of theological self-understanding, is quite true, regardless of the truth or falsity of certain empirical-historical claims of Luke, such as that Paul studied in Jerusalem with Gamaliel (Acts 22:3). The theological significance of Acts' proposal is that it might enable the church today to reclaim its rootedness in and indebtedness to Judaism as well as to reconstitute itself in solidarity with the people Israel, for whom it has so long preached contempt. A proposal's interest for us and for our self-understanding as Christians is not limited to questions of its truthfulness, although obviously there are situations where lack of truthfulness will detract from interest.

Contemporizing of Tradition

In James Sanders' "canonical criticism," canonical texts are always "contemporized" traditions. This means that interpretation proceeds on the model of a conversation with the text, and the logic of conversation is the logic of question and answer. The interpreter asks questions of the texts and the text, in its turn, puts questions to the interpreter. The interpreter goes to the text with an interest, and the fact that the interpreter goes to *this* text (e.g., the Bible) shows that the interpreter is in this text's "effective history" or "field of force."[47] But what Sanders' expression "contemporized traditions" makes us remember is that the text itself was an answer to a question, a question that must be surfaced if the text is to be understood.

Different texts, written at different times and places, to differing circumstances, seek to answer different questions. As new questions arise, new answers are forthcoming. These new answers, or texts, are contemporized to new situations. Although there is no scholarly certainty on the point, there is evidence that during his lifetime Jesus and his disciples understood themselves as concerned exclusively with "the lost sheep of the house of Israel," and not at all with Gentiles. Matthew preserves traditions according to which, when Jesus sent out the twelve, he charged them to "go nowhere among the Gentiles, and enter no town of the Samaritans, but go rather to the lost sheep of the house of Israel" (10:5). Many scholars, including some process theologians, regard the "exclusivity logion" as authentic.[48]

The early church that produced the scriptures was able to retain these evidences of its early "limitation" to Jews in the very document that ends in the Great Commission to "make disciples of all nations" (Matt. 28:19). It should be noted that the term "all nations" is *panta ta ethne*, "all the Gentiles;" there is no mention of Jews in the Great Commission. The "only to the house of Israel" passages reflect a question and answer from the early part of the first century; the Great Commission reflects a question and answer from the latter part of the first century. In between, the tradition had been creatively transformed in continuity with itself but "without the obligation of *conformity*" to the past; it could give a new answer to a new question arising later "without the *rejection* of tradition."[49] Process thought understands creative transformation as the rendering of incompatibilities into sub-contrasts within a more concrete whole. Therefore the apparent contradiction between the limitations of the Jesus movement to the house of Israel and the calling of the church to go to all the Gentiles is not considered a problem. In each case, tradition is contemporized to a different situation and made to answer a different question. In each case, the mission is to make known the promise and command of God to each and all: in the one case to *all* the house of Israel, including its lost sheep, in the other to *all* the peoples.

This latter comment discloses, by the way, that a relatively clear statement of a norm of appropriateness need not be taken to imply that its authors hold that there is an absolute, unchanging essence to Christianity. What we hold is that the meaning of such words as "all" is itself contemporized to different situations at different times and places. Abstractly, "all" means "the whole of," with none left out. Concretely, "all" can grow in meaning. That God loves "all," in the early Jesus movement, meant that God loved the whole of the house of Israel, including especially its "lost sheep." Later in the Jesus movement, "all" took on a larger meaning; it came to be seen that God's love for all had to be taken in the light of God's initial promise to Abraham that his seed would be a light to the Gentiles: God loves even or especially the lost Gentile sheep. In our own time we have clearly learned that the "all" whom God loves is a rather larger "all" than we had previously taken it to be; now it includes especially *women* and *blacks* and the *barrio-dwellers* of Latin America, to name but a few. For some Christians, after a long tradition inclining them to the contrary, even *Jews* are especially loved by God. This does not mean that there is an absolute, unchanging essence to Christianity. Rather, it illustrates the distinction that Schubert Ogden develops, from Stephen Toulmin, between the "field-invariant force" of criteria of appropriateness and adequacy and their "field-dependent standards," which Ogden later refers to as their "context-invariant" and "context-dependent" aspects.[50] It is sufficient, in our view, to say that the "force" of such criteria is "context-transferrable," without getting too worked up over how universally invariant they are.

A similar relationship exists, David Lull suggests, between the letters of Paul and the letter of James. James, writing some time after Paul, was aware of Christians who held that "faith without works" is salvific (2:14). In this, they seem to have thought that they agreed with Paul, who had argued that justification is by faith "apart from works prescribed by the law" (Romans 3:28). But in their time and place, the question that Paul was trying to answer was no longer being asked, and the situation that he had addressed was no longer pressing. Paul was striving to gain an equal place for his Gentile followers within the Jesus movement without requiring them to submit to the ritual practices of circumcision and the food laws, practices that served as the "identity markers" or "membership badges" of the Jewish people, and which to Paul indicated that the grace of God is not available outside the boundaries of that people.[51] In James's time, Christianity was, as Lull says, "well on the way to becoming a Gentile religion, separate from Judaism," and there was little if any pressure to conform to Jewish ritual requirements. Now the question about "faith without works" was being raised by people "whose lives exhibited moral laxity."[52] In this situation, James could not possibly be satisfied with a hermeneutic of "mere conformity to tradition," because such conformity was precisely what had produced the "heresy" of thinking that faith need not be active in love. So, James "contemporized" tradition, in a way that was more faithful than conforming to it would have been, and transformed it to enable it to answer the new question.

Summary

By way of a quick review, what we have tried to do here is to lay out the basic, introductory groundwork of our approach to process hermeneutics. We began with the need for a norm of appropriateness, described the nature of scripture itself as an instance of tradition—the final precipitate of a long process of revision and reinterpretation and subject to further reinterpretation—sought to lay bare scripture's self-critical hermeneutic and to adopt it as our norm of appropriateness, indicated why a concern for credibility is of critical importance to the gospel itself (hardly just to be well adapted to "modernity"), and sought to show how process hermeneutics tries to avoid the fallacy of misplaced concreteness by contextualizing Jesus and Paul, reading scripture concretely rather than only abstractly, by looking at texts as proposals and at the contemporizing of tradition.

Process hermeneuticists are widely agreed that ours is not a "jealous" hermeneutic. Other hermeneutical methods, such as Bultmann's demythologizing and existential interpretation, are welcome and affirmed for their contributions to the hermeneutical task. We prefer to speak of "de-literalizing" rather than "demythologizing," because of the inevitable fuss that is kicked up whenever the word "demythologizing" is uttered. We also prefer it because we believe it more appropriate to Bultmann's intent. The problem is not myth or mythology but literalized myth. While we do not propose to argue it here, for want of space, we suggest that Bultmann's concern with myth was that its language could invite a literalizing interpretation that precisely misses the deeper truth that myth can impart. Nor do we shy away from "existential interpretation," because, as we argued in an earlier chapter, we find this quite compatible with Whitehead's own strong emphasis on "decision" as the very meaning of actuality and the basis of givenness. "Decision" is what, in Whitehead, replaces the category of "substance" and makes the latter unnecessary. There is a profound existentialism in Whitehead. Nor will existential interpretation leave one lost in the quagmires of privacy, not unless one engages in it while presuming a nonsocial, nontemporal, substantialist self, which is precisely what process thought does not presuppose. So we see no problem with existential interpretation, but welcome it. The existence we are interpreting is a process-relational existence.

Also, because of the social, temporal, historical nature of process thought and process hermeneutics, we welcome and use the various methods of ideology criticism and political interpretation.

As a matter of fact, much of what has gone before in this chapter is unintelligible without at least the presupposition of at least some of these. Both feminists and people concerned with overcoming Christian anti-Judaism find much promise in the process/relational approach to hermeneutics. We have not concentrated on these various matters in this chapter for the simple reason that we have been trying to highlight what is distinctive, not exclusive, to process hermeneutics and, at the same time, to provide examples of process hermeneutics at work. Now we turn our attention to the more directly homiletical nature of the task of appropriating scripture for preaching.

Notes

¹Readers interested in orienting themselves to process hermeneutics are referred to the discussions found in the following sources: "New Testament Interpretation from a Process Perspective," *Journal of the American Academy of Religion,* Vol. 47, No. 1 (1979) and "Old Testament Interpretation from a Process Perspective," *Semeia,* Vol. 24 (1982), and William A. Beardslee's essay, "Recent Hermeneutics and Process Thought," *Process Studies,* Vol. 12, No. 2 (1982), pp. 65-76. Also helpful for the questions it raises is David H. Kelsey's "The Theological Use of Scripture in Process Hermeneutics," *Process Studies,* Vol. 13, No. 3 (1983), pp. 181-188, as is David J. Lull's introductory article, "What Is 'Process Hermeneutics'?", *Process Studies,* Vol. 13, No. 3 (1983), pp. 189-201.

²Barry A. Woodbridge, "An Assessment and Prospectus for a Process Hermeneutics," *Journal of the American Academy of Religion,* Vol. 47, No. 1 (March 1979), p. 126.

³*Ibid.,* p. 126.

⁴Schubert M. Ogden, "Toward a New Theism," in *Process Philosophy and Christian Thought,* ed. Delwin Brown, Ralph E. James, Jr., and Gene Reeves (Indianapolis: Bobbs-Merrill, 1971), p. 173.

⁵James Barr, *The Scope and Authority of the Bible* (Philadelphia: Westminster Press, 1980), p. 58.

⁶*Ibid.,* p. 59.

⁷*Ibid.,* p. 60.

⁸*Ibid.*

⁹Barry A. Woodbridge, "An Assessment and Prospectus for a Process Hermeneutic," *Journal of the American Academy of Religion,* Vol. 47, No. 1 (March 1979), p. 124.

¹⁰See Paul J. Achtemeier, "*Omne verbum sonat*: The New Testament and

the Oral Environment of Late Western Antiquity," *Journal of Biblical Literature,* Vol. 109, No. 1 (Spring 1990), pp. 3-27.

[11]James A. Sanders, *Canon and Community* (Philadelphia: Fortress Press, 1984), p. xvii.

[12]*Ibid.,* p. 27.

[13]*Ibid.,* p. 28.

[14]*Ibid.,* p. 31.

[15]Trible is cited in Sanders, *ibid.,* p. 41.

[16]*Ibid.,* p. 46; the following description of Sanders' canonical criticism follows his treatment on pp. 51-59.

[17]*Ibid.,* p. 54; italics Sanders'.

[18]E. P. Sanders, *Paul, the Law, and the Jewish People* (Philadelphia: Fortress Press, 1983), p. 113.

[19]See, e.g., Schubert M. Ogden, *On Theology* (San Francisco: Harper & Row, 1986), pp. 4-6.

[20]This discussion is dependent on Schubert M. Ogden's discussion of the same passages in *Rockefeller Chapel Sermons,* comp. Donovan E. Smucker (Chicago: The University of Chicago Press, 1966), pp. 98-109.

[21]Alfred North Whitehead, *Religion in the Making* (New York: Meridian Books, 1960), p. 30.

[22]H. Richard Niebuhr, *The Meaning of Revelation* (New York: Macmillan, 1941), p. 93f.

[23]Whitehead, *Process and Reality,* p. 7.

[24]Whitehead, *Modes of Thought,* p. 36.

[25]*Ibid.,* p. 36f.

[26]*Ibid.,* p. 37. In *Fallible Forms and Symbols,* Bernard Meland comments that "there is language in silences; and in the spaces between words" (p. 30). There can only be "silence" in spoken language.

[27]Paul J. Achtemeier, *"Omne Verbum Sonat,"* p. 3.

[28]*Ibid.*

[29]*Ibid.,* p. 15.

[30]*Ibid.*

[31]*Ibid.,* p. 17.

[32]Whitehead, *Modes of Thought,* p. 39.

[33]Augustine, *On Christian Doctrine,* tr. D. W. Robertson, Jr. (Indianapolis: Bobbs-Merrill, 1958), pp. 79, 81.

[34]Charles R. Blaisdell, who coined the expression "tone of voice exegesis," provides an example of its possibilities in "Speak to the Heart of Jerusalem: The 'Conversational' Structure of Deutero-Isaiah," *Encounter,* Vol. 52, No. 1 (Winter 1991). The following application of tone of voice exegesis to the story of the healing of the centurion's servant was made by Blaisdell in his sermon "A Gruff God?" preached at Christian Theological Seminary on October 4, 1988.

[35]Blaisdell, "A Gruff God," p. 3.

[36]*Ibid.*

[37]See Clark M. Williamson, *Has God Rejected His People?* (Nashville: Abingdon Press, 1982), chap. 1. See also Bernard J. Lee, *The Galilean Jewishness of Jesus* (New York: Paulist Press, 1988).

[38]For a clear definition and application of the criterion of dissimilarity, see Norman Perrin, *Rediscovering the Teaching of Jesus* (New York: Harper & Row, 1976), p. 43.

[39]Theodore J. Weeden, "The Potential and Promise of a Process Hermeneutic," *Encounter*, Vol. 36, No. 4 (Autumn 1975), p. 318.

[40]For Meland's "communal ground of being," see *Fallible Forms and Symbols, passim*; for locating Jesus in context as a corrective to Christology, see Williamson, *Has God Rejected His People?*, chap. 1.

[41]Whitehead, *Process and Reality*, p. 256.

[42]*Ibid.*

[43]*Ibid.*, p. 258.

[44]*Ibid.*, p. 259.

[45]David J. Lull develops this aspect of process hermeneutics: "What Is 'Process Hermeneutics'?", *Process Studies* Vol. 13, No. 3 (Fall 1983), p. 193.

[46]*Ibid.*

[47]The relation between Hans Georg Gadamer's "effective history" (*Wirkungsgeschichte*) and John B. Cobb's "field of force" was argued by Williamson in "Process Hermeneutics and Christianity's Post-Holocaust Reinterpretation of Itself," *Process Studies*, Vol. 12, No. 2 (Summer 1982), p. 81.

[48]See, e.g., Bernard J. Lee, *The Galilean Jewishness of Jesus*, p. 67ff.

[49]Lull, "What Is 'Process Hermeneutics'?", p. 195.

[50]See the discussion in Ogden, *The Reality of God*, p. 38ff., and *On Theology*, p. 5f.

[51]See James D. G. Dunn, *Jesus, Paul and the Law* (Louisville: Westminster/ John Knox Press, 1990), p. 11f.

[52]Lull, "What Is 'Process Hermeneutics'?", p. 196.

Chapter 5

The Interpretation of Biblical Texts

A process approach to hermeneutics "regards biblical texts, precisely in their function as *proposed* ways of understanding (aspects of) objective reality, as important for the readers' 'forms of subjectivity.'"[1] That is, each text of the Bible makes its own witness. Each passage presents a view of God and of the world and of their interrelationship that readers are asked to accept as authoritative. One of the preacher's tasks is to help the congregation discover how the consideration of a text can enhance and enlarge the congregation's sense of Christian identity and mission in the world. This can be a complicated task. To be sure, the whole of the Bible deals with the relationship of God and the world. But the Bible is not a single book in which every proposition coheres with every other proposition. It is more like a library that contains a wide variety of propositions on the meaning of life in the world with God. On a given topic, some of the voices in the Bible disagree.

At least on the surface, many of the perspectives found in the Bible are welcome. They picture a loving, gracious, believable, moral relationship between God and the world and they advocate a loving, gracious, moral community within the world. However, some texts advocate views of God, the cosmos and human community that are unloving, ungracious, and immoral. If the preacher simply reproduces the content of a given biblical text on Sunday morning, the sermon might be an important, timely gospel message, or it could leave the listeners lost in the mists of antiquity. The sermon could misrepresent God, be unbelievable, and even sanction human or environmental abuse. From one Sunday to another, the pastor might preach sermons that are mutually contradictory.

We preachers need a way to deal with biblical texts that allows the consideration of the text to be illuminating and instructive for us but does not make us prisoners of the text with its theology and worldview. A process hermeneutics lets us respect the text for what it is and for what it says, and yet lets us view the text in the light of a coherent theological system that seeks to make sense in (and of) the world. Indeed, a process conceptuality can often help us make interpretive moves that yield positive, freedom-enhancing meaning in our encounter with the text when (on the surface) the text seems to be theologically and morally bankrupt, or intractably difficult.[2]

In the previous chapter we sketched a framework for conceptualizing how process hermeneutics can guide us in interpreting biblical texts. In this chapter we offer a methodology that can help preachers engage specific passages from the Bible in a disciplined way. In particular we show how the norms of appropriateness to the gospel and credibility are an essential part of preparation for preaching. We also draw upon representative notions from process thought to illustrate ways in which this worldview can be a practical help in reinterpreting biblical texts for our time.[3]

We focus on three moments on the path of sermon preparation: exegesis—>theological analysis—>meaning for today. In the moment of exegesis, the preacher identifies the full range of the claims of the text. In theological analysis the preacher reflects on the claims of the text in the light of the norms of appropriateness, credibility, and moral plausibility. The preacher also reflects on these norms in the light of the claims of the text. In the last step, the preacher makes a mutual, critical correlation between the text and the contemporary congregation. At what points does the text enrich our understanding and practice of Christian life? At what points do our understanding and practice of Christian life enrich the text? Are there points at which the witness of the text is incomplete and even mistaken? Are there points at which the text causes us to see that our understanding of Christian faith and life is incomplete and mistaken? In actual practice, of course, these three moments seldom unfold sequentially as distinct occasions. The tasks of each moment often intermingle with those of others.

When following this path, the preacher seeks to enter into honest conversation with the text, the rest of the canon, the tradition of the church, and the experience and reason of the contemporary church and world.[4] Since conversation is the model, the preacher may expect to be surprised from time to time. The text may challenge the preacher and the listening community and bring about a change of mind, heart, and practice.

Exegesis

The purpose of the preacher's exegesis is to recover a text's witness concerning the situation of the world, God, and God's relationship to the world. The integrity of the text is a fundamental issue. In a genuine conversation, we want to hear what others have to say and not simply what we wish they would say. A great temptation of biblical interpreters is to read the text in the light of their own agendas, values, and practices. The name for this is eisegesis: consciously or unconsciously hearing the text say what the interpreter wishes it so say, even when the text does not so speak. Thus, a first step in working with a text is to be suspicious of how one's exegetical and theological predispositions are influenced by political ideology, economic and social prejudice, ethnic and racial sensitivities, national and international loyalties, personal moral values, and phobias. Awareness of these inbuilt persuasions will help us not be blindly controlled by them as we try to listen to the text. The rule is: Be suspicious.[5] In any case, an interpreter informed by process theology has great freedom to let the text have its own say. Of course, the process thinker regards the text as an other with its own inherent value. But more, process theology does not require the Bible to back up its ideas in order for those ideas to be considered valid.[6] Thus, the interpreter need not twist the text in order to get it to conform to some orthodoxy. The text is always free to be itself. Even when a text voices incomplete or mistaken ideas, it can be a stimulus for creative transformation.

Many contemporary biblical scholars remind us that a text may speak more than one word. It may have such a "surplus of meaning" that we should be cautious of thinking we have found its one and only meaning.[7] Another interpreter may hear a word with a different accent. In other circumstances I myself may be sensitive to yet another possibility of meaning. But every meaning derived from a text must be a meaning that legitimately comes from the text itself.

For the preparation of the Christian sermon, the most important part of exegesis is the identification of the text's theological witness. This witness is comprised of the claims of the text regarding God, the situation of the world, the relationship of God to the world, and the response of human beings and nature to God. The following three questions provide a convenient way to clarify the witness of the text. The answers to these questions may not always appear in a single pericope but can nearly always be found in its larger context or in the worldview from which the text originated. We shall illustrate the practical value of this approach by applying the questions to Mark 1:21–28, the exorcism of the person with the unclean spirit in the synagogue at Capernaum.

1. *What is the situation of the world (especially the communities of humankind and nature) presupposed by this text?* The gospel of Mark is based upon an apocalyptic worldview. Norman Perrin and Dennis Duling describe Mark as an apocalyptic drama; apocalyptic theology is given expression in narrative form.[8] The apocalyptic worldview flowered when the Jewish people experienced intense social unrest and oppression in the years 300 B.C.E. to 200 C.E. During these years, Palestine was continuously in turmoil and, for the most part, controlled by Gentiles. Many Jewish people suffered. Questions asserted themselves again and again. "Why is there so much suffering and evil in the world? If God is truly powerful and faithful, why do we languish? What will God do to demonstrate God's righteousness, to be faithful to God's own character and to what God has promised?" Apocalyptic theologians answered these questions and accounted for the difficult situation of the world by claiming that the world had been created good. Genesis 1 and 2 preserve the memory of the world as Eden (which means "Delight"). The world was as God meant for it to be: a place in which all relationships were full and right. All things acknowledged the Lord as God. But then, one created thing, Satan, sought the honor

that properly belonged to God. Human beings joined in this quest. As a result, God the all-powerful placed the world under a curse (Genesis 3). After the fall, God permitted evil to flourish.

Apocalyptic theologians believed that history was divided into two consecutive ages. The first age (in which the apocalyptic heroes were still living) was called by such names as the "old age," "this age," "this world," "the realm [RSV: kingdom] of this world." During the old age, Satan and the demons were ever attempting to wrestle persons, communities, institutions, and nature itself away from God. This old order was a time of sin, brokenness, disease, violence, social oppression, enmity between humankind and nature, and death. Apocalyptic thinkers believed that the events of this world were predetermined (at least in a general way) and that God had already decided to intervene at a certain (but not completely known) time. The intervention would be a great historical cataclysm in which God would act as a cosmic warrior, invading the old age and destroying the power of Satan. God would restore all things to their intended purpose. The new world would be much like the world of Genesis 1 and 2. This new age is called by such names as "the realm [RSV: kingdom] of God" and "the age to come."[9]

In Mark 1:21–28, this situation is represented by the man with the unclean spirit. He is not responsible for himself but is under the power of a demon. As a demoniac he is a miniature of the situation of the world as a whole.[10] Antoinette Wire describes this situation as a closed circle or a fixed mold. The person is trapped inside the situation.[11]

2. *What is the relationship of God to the world in this text?* God does not appear directly in Mark 1:21–28, but Jesus appears as the divine agent ("the Holy One of God") who has *authority* sufficient to confront the demon and cast it out of the man. For Mark, this indicates that God has begun to invade the old age and release it from bondage to Satan through the ministry of Jesus (cf. 1:14–15). Power and conflict are continuous underlying issues in the Gospel of Mark: God, through Jesus, is in constant conflict with Satan. One purpose of Mark is to reveal that the power (authority) of God is stronger than that of Satan. In this text, God is the exorcist who frees the world from the powers that bind it.

3. *What is the desired response of humankind and nature to the presence of God in the world?* The response of the crowd to the

exorcism is a clue to the response desired from the hearer. "They were all amazed, and they kept on asking one another, 'What is this? A new teaching—with authority! He commands even the unclean spirits, and they obey him'" (1:27). The appeal is for the listeners to recognize the exorcising authority of Jesus. What Jesus is pictured as doing in the synagogue at Capernaum, the risen Jesus continues to do through the church. They can welcome this activity, and willingly let themselves be exorcised. Indeed, they can become disciples of Jesus whereas those who oppose Jesus are enemies of God.

The witness of a text often exists on two levels: a *surface witness* and a *deeper witness*. The surface witness is the meaning of a text at the simplest and most obvious level in the light of its own worldview, language, and imagery. In the case of Mark 1:21–28, the text would have us believe that the world is inhabited by Satan and demons and that Jesus frees people and institutions from these binding realities.

However, according to David Buttrick, the field of concern of a text is often deeper than its surface meaning.[12] The field of concern is the larger theological issue within which the text is to be understood. Perhaps an analogy will help make the point. The symptom of an illness is very important (especially to the patient), and it deserves to be treated, but until the source of the symptom is itself treated, it will recur. A text is often a symptom of a deeper theological concern.[13]

In Mark 1:21–28, the deeper issue is the righteousness of God and the manifestation of that righteousness in the face of monstrous evil. Mark pictures evil in the form of the demons and Satan who bind life. How can God be righteous, and faithful to God's own character and promises, when evil is so prominent? The answer is that the power of God is stronger than the power of Satan as demonstrated in the exorcism at Capernaum. The exorcism is a "mini-apocalypse," which shows in the case of the individual Capurnian that God can be trusted to exorcise the whole world through the coming apocalyptic event. Based on the evidence of the exorcisms, the cross, and the resurrection, the community can wait in hope for the full and final revelation of God's righteousness. This little text is a piece of one of the most penetrating problems in the Bible and of Christian theology to this day. Its particular theological slant is apocalyptic but its ultimate concern goes beyond apocalyptic theology.

The exegetical task is not only to engage the text through the various critical disciplines. It is also to identify the witness of the text in both its surface and deeper meanings. Ultimately, the whole text must become the subject of theological analysis. Careful exegesis sometimes causes us to look afresh at texts. Exegesis can cause us to radically revise our understanding of a text. A text is often "understood" in the church in two arenas: (1) the popular arena, which is frequently naive and informed mainly by individual opinion, barbershop conversation, and the authority of a local Bible study group; (2) the scholarly arena, which is informed by critical study. Sometimes these ways of interpreting a text are very different, and one line of interpretation can exist without its holders being aware of the other. Therefore it is important for the preacher to be aware of the ways in which the meanings of a text are assumed in the congregation to which the sermon will be preached. In the sermon, preachers will often find it helpful to state the opinion that is about to be revised. We look now at some sample texts that are being exegetically reinterpreted in our time.

Genesis 1:1–2:2 contains the influential verses 26–31 which assert that human beings, made in the image of God, have been given dominion over the earth and everything that creeps upon it. Popularly, this has often been taken to mean that we have been given the authority to do whatever we want to the earth.[14] This view has led human beings to exploit the earth and other human beings. The more we regard nature as a set of things to be manipulated, the more we regard other kinds of human beings as part of "nature" and similarly disposable.

However, our understanding of the text has been revised such that to be made in the image of God means to exercise dominion in one's own sphere of influence in the *way* in which God exercises dominion in the whole cosmos. What does it mean to say that God exercises dominion? Here, Genesis 1:1 is crucial. The creation sequence begins with the description of the world as a watery, violent chaos in which relationship and order are impossible. God exercises dominion by restraining the power of chaos and by creating order and relationality. As the creation drama comes to a close, it is clear that God exercises dominion by creating the conditions for right relationship among the natural world, animals, and human beings.

In the scenario of Genesis 1, women and men live in mutual partnership with no hint of hierarchy. All things are together in mutual support. Indeed, the animal and human species do not even use one another as food; they eat only plants that reproduce themselves. Animals and human beings are vegetarian; no relationship is ended by death.[15] Humankind exercises dominion in the world by observing the conditions in which all things can exist together in the quality of mutually supportive relationship.[16] This way of thinking about Genesis 1 differs from that which sees dominion as license for exploiting the earth and animals. The notions of community and relationality are at the very heart of the Hebrew and Christian conceptions of the world and human community and come to play a key role in the Bible's thinking about covenant, justice, and the rule of God. Genesis 1 and 2 is a picture of a just and sustainable world.

At one time it was widely believed that the Bible is, from start to finish, an imprimatur upon patriarchy. The Bible generally accepts patriarchal visions of human relationship and speaks of God in patriarchal language. The latter is especially important since our vision of God establishes the pattern for human relationships. Yet, revisers have discovered that a number of texts present models of God that are decidedly feminine in character and texts that are quite egalitarian in their vision of the role of women in marriage, outside of marriage, and in the larger life of Israel and the church. These texts have the effect of subverting the patriarchal view of the world.

The book of Ruth is frequently taken as a gentle love story between Ruth and Boaz. However, when read against the cultural assumptions of the period in which the book was composed, we can see that it contains a strikingly different point of view with respect to the possibilities available to women. According to Phyllis Trible, in the whole of the Hebrew Bible, only the behavior of Abraham matches the radical behavior of the woman Ruth, "but then he had a call from God (Genesis 12:1–5)."

> Divine promise motivated and sustained his leap of faith. Besides, Abraham was a man, with a wife and other possessions to accompany him. Ruth stands alone; she

possesses nothing. No God has called her; no deity has promised her blessing; no human being has come to her aid. She lives and chooses without a support group and she knows that the fruit of her decision may well be the emptiness of rejection, indeed, of death. Consequently, not even Abraham's leap of faith surpasses Ruth's. And there is more. Not only has Ruth broken with family, country and faith, she has also reversed sexual allegiance. A young woman has committed herself to the life of an old woman rather than to the search for a husband, and she has made this commitment not "until death do us part," but beyond death. One female has chosen a female in a world where life depends upon men. There is no more radical decision in all the memories of Israel.[17]

This pattern is manifest throughout the book of Ruth and serves to criticize patriarchy. Trible concludes that the struggle of Ruth and Naomi becomes a mode of divine activity "redeeming curse through blessing."[18]

One of the most systematic revisions currently under way in biblical scholarship is focused on *Paul's relationship with Judaism* and particularly on *his attitude toward the law*. Hitherto, we have tended to read Paul's statements about the law as condemning it. According to Paul, we were told by the inherited paradigm, the effect of the law on human life was extremely negative and the law was something from which humanity needed to be redeemed. Christ, as interpreted by this Paul, was the way by which people were freed from obedience to the stern taskmaster-law and the only way whereby the grace of God was made available to the human family. Faith in Christ thereby renders the law obsolete. Paul, though a Jew, is represented as rejecting one of the quintessential marks of Judaism. This interpretation both reflects and reinforces Christian anti-Jewish ideology.

A strong wave in recent scholarship, however, seeks to revise this view radically. Instead of interpreting Paul in opposition to Judaism it sees him as a faithful Jew who views Christ as the confirmation of God's promises to the Gentiles to bring them into God's own household. Where Jews relate to God primarily through Torah (understood as God's gracious gift), Gentiles relate to God through Christ. Henceforth, the household of God contains two parallel families: the people Israel and the church. Paul's special vocation in the service of God is to spread the gospel among the Gentiles.[19]

However, Paul's ministry was frustrated by some who sought for Gentile converts to adopt Jewish customs. This, for instance, is the case at Galatia where Paul addresses the subject of the Gentile Christian and the law in detail and with considerable passion. Galatians 2:15–21 is a key passage in this discussion. The received exegetical tradition would see this passage as declaring the end of the validity of the law, and indeed, as declaring Judaism itself to be invalid as a means of receiving God's grace and as a channel for faithful service to God.

Lloyd Gaston, who argues for a revised understanding of Paul and Judaism as sketched above, argues quite differently that this passage seeks not to denigrate Judaism or Jewish Christianity but only to justify the practice of Gentiles coming to God through Christ without becoming Jews. Gaston's argument is complex and depends on a close reading of Galatians in the light of primary Jewish texts that illustrate Jewish thought at the time of Paul. The argument hinges on the following details. First, the passage has the literary character of a *propositio*, a section common in Greco-Roman rhetoric whose purpose was to sum up the preceding material and state the main idea that was the subject of the document. In this case, Paul's primary intention is to defend his "gospel to the uncircumcised" as well as to interpret the event in Antioch discussed in 2:1–14.[20]

A key phrase in the passage "works of the law" does not appear in any other Jewish literature to the time of Paul. On the basis of a close reading of the uses of "law" in Jewish texts contemporaneous with Paul, Gaston concludes that "law" is used in several different ways. These range from "torah"—law as the gracious gift and revelation of God as part of the covenant with the Hebrews at Sinai—to a use in some apocalyptic texts in which law functions to condemn Gentiles. Gaston concludes that in Galatians 2:15–21, the phrase "works of the law" "does not refer to Jews keeping commandments but to God punishing Gentiles."[21] The basis of this view is a little-known use of "law" in the apocalyptic literature of early Judaism in "which the law actively works in the Gentile world to create a situation from which people need redemption. Here, outside the context of covenant, law exercises retribution for human sinfulness in a process called 'wrath.'"[22] The passage is fundamentally not about Jews who seek to justify themselves by doing works of the law but about Gentiles who, apart from God, stand under the wrath of this aspect of the working of the law.

Still another hinge is Paul's use of the first-person pronoun in the passage. Paul speaks not of Jewish Christians but of Gentile Christians. He uses the first person, perhaps because he has identified so closely with the Gentiles to whom he has been commissioned to preach, that he can speak as if he were himself a Gentile. The Gentiles are the sinners of verses 16–17. This conclusion is especially important to verse 19 where Paul views himself as a Gentile under the condemnation of the law. Paul, at least in language used here, has effectively abandoned the justification that was available to him through the covenant at Sinai, and which is still operative among Jews.[23]

A final hinge is Gaston's retranslation of 2:21 as follows: "I do not set at nought the grace of God; for since through law is the righteousness of God, consequently Christ has died as a free gift."[24] Here Paul uses "law" in another sense common to early Judaism with reference to the revelation of God's righteousness and salvation now extended to Gentiles. The point is that Christ's death and resurrection are the means through which God's grace comes to Gentiles and to this the law is a witness. Paul's identification with the Gentile community does not make illegitimate the Sinai covenant through which God's grace was made known to Jews.

Revision of traditional exegetical conclusions needs always to be tested in the wider community of interpreters. But when tested and verified it can prove very welcome to Christians of our day.

Theological Analysis

When the witness of the text is clearly in view, the preacher then engages in theological analysis of the witness of the text. Does the text tell the truth about God? About the world? About God's relationship with the world? Does it call the congregation to enlarge its view of God, God's activity in the world, and its vision for the human or natural communities? To analyze the witness of the text, we draw upon the criteria for theological evaluation articulated in the previous chapter: *appropriateness to the gospel* and *credibility* (both intellectual and moral).[25] These yield two questions that can be asked of the witness of any text, and in their light the preacher evaluates the claims of the text.[26]

A caveat: As is well known among preachers and biblical scholars, a biblical text that is appropriate and credible often challenges the preacher and the congregation to broaden or refocus their vision of God, of God's relationship to the world, or the response of the world to God. As William Beardslee and his colleagues put it:

> What this illustrates is that we can encounter the biblical proposal that God is immanently and inwardly active in all events as a challenge to the mechanical understanding of events on which the dominant modern paradigm of the universe is based, and in terms of which most theologians think about the world. More important than striving for coherence or conformity between these two views—for example by pointing to events of indeterminacy and open-ness in small-scale events in modern physics, though this is certainly to the point—is the biblical conviction that all such events have value and carry value, since they too embody the divine presence. This contribution from the biblical side can become a challenge to rethink the dualism, determinism and mechanism that run so deeply through our modern thinking about the world and that make belief in God increasingly problematic.[27]

Even a biblical text that may not be wholly appropriate or intelligible may challenge the preacher and congregation to enlarge or refocus their vision. Thus, we need to remember that the relationship between text and preacher is dialectical. What we think is appropriate and credible must be open to challenge in a genuine conversation with the text.

Before the criteria of appropriateness and credibility can be employed, they must be informed by a clear understanding of the content of the gospel, a clear understanding of the contemporary world (and especially of how things happen in the world), and a clear understanding of the nature of God's power and of the ways in which God acts in the world. We find these in a process approach to the Christian faith.

1. *Is the witness of the text appropriate to the gospel?* The gospel is the good news of God's unconditional love for each and every created thing and the command of God that justice be done for each and every created thing. God's pure, unbounded love is to be shown to each and every created being in each and every relationship and situation. When the witness of a text assumes God's love for each and all, the text is appropriate to the gospel. But when the text denies that God loves any created thing, it is inappropriate to the gospel. In some cases, the witness of a text is altogether appropriate or altogether inappropriate. But in many instances a text makes a mixed witness that affirms God's love for some but denies it for others.

The isolated unit of Mark 1:21–28 would seem to be appropriate to the gospel. For the text shows the active, liberating power of God's love working on behalf of the person with the unclean spirit; the pericope does not appear to deny God's love to any.[28] In the apocalyptic model, however, exorcism is a violent act in which the stronger one overpowers the demon. Thus, this is a story of God's brute force overwhelming the demon. It pictures God's power as coercive, whereas process theology regards God's power as persuasive; nor in our experience is there any analogy for God acting in the way characterized in the text.

A monopolar gospel of unlimited love could be misconstrued as license for unlimited immorality. But the dipolar character of the gospel guards against this. For the gospel is the news of God's unconditional love *and* God's call for universal justice. In the Christian tradition, justice is the quality of all created things living together in right relationship (as presumed in Genesis 1 and 2). The gospel claims that God loves each and every created thing and that each and every being is to be treated as if it mattered to God. This is a meta-ethical reason to be moral. Even when we violate this norm, the gospel insists that God never writes us off. Nor does God write off any person, community or situation. Instead, God continues to offer the possibility of saying "yes" to God's love for self and neighbor. In this sense, God's judgments truly are *righteous*, for God wills to do what is right, what is consistent with God's own character.

2. *Is the witness of the text credible?* Is the witness of the text worthy of belief in the light of our experience and understanding of the world and its operation? Is it consistent with what we otherwise believe concerning God, the gospel and the ways in which God exercises power in the world? Does the text prescribe or presume the moral treatment of all concerned? Of course, the other side of the coin is that interpreters may have their views of the world, and their understanding of their experience, enlarged and challenged by the text. Yet, the church can hardly expect its witness to be taken seriously if it asks people to engage in the willful suspension of disbelief. The preacher can learn to ask the question of whether the text (or some aspect of the text) is true or not true in the light of our experience and observation of life. However, we need to exercise caution at this point. Surface elements of a text may be unintelligible to us, whereas deeper elements may be intelligible. At the deeper level, the experiences that are common to the biblical world and to our culture may go by different names in each cultural milieu. Process theology often comes to our aid as it helps us identify this deeper dimension.

Mark 1:21–28 is centered in the exorcism of a man with an unclean spirit. In the mind of the first century, an unclean spirit was an identifiable being that lived in the universe in a way similar to a person. A demon had its own identity, personality and will. Demons would willfully possess people (or institutions) as they did the person in the synagogue at Capernaum, robbing the person of autonomy. A person could be released from demons through exorcism—the displacement of the power of the demons by a power greater than that of demons. In the incident at the synagogue at Capernaum, Jesus is pictured in the role of an exorcist who has behind him the power of the new age in which God breaks the crippling power of the demons.

At the surface level, this text is simply not intelligible to people today. We do not believe in first-century style demons or exorcism. But at a deeper level, the text is much more intelligible, especially in light of the emergence of apocalyptic theology (which we sketched above). The demons appear in Jewish literature in the fully developed form after 300 B.C. to personify the experience of evil characteristic of the old age. Exorcism is a demonstration that the new age is coming. Life is not a closed circle but is now a "circle burst open, a mold broken," with new and exciting possibilities.[29]

We, too, experience the crippling of life. Where the first-century writer would explain the binding of life by pointing to demons, we would point to other causes that result in binding. Walter Wink writes that the powers of today have an inner aspect and an outer aspect.

> As the inner aspect, they are the spirituality of institutions, the "within" of corporate structures and systems, the inner essence of the outer organizations of power. As the outer aspect, they are political systems, appointed officials, the "chair" of an organization, laws—in short, all the tangible manifestations which power takes. Every power tends to have a visible pole, an outer form—be it a church, a nation or an economy—and an invisible pole, an inner spirit or driving force that animates, legitimates and regulates its physical manifestation in the world.[30]

When any such power commands absolute devotion, it is idolatrous and demonic. For example, alcohol becomes demonic when it so possesses people as to turn them into alcoholics dedicated above all else to alcohol. Racism is a systemic demon that causes large numbers of people to live as if imprisoned.[31]

People and situations in our world can experience release from the "possessions" that bind them. While Jesus no longer walks the earth as portrayed in the Markan narrative, the aim for human life that he represents (and which is represented by the image of the realm of God) still attracts us.[32] When we respond in faith and trust, the quality of our lives does change. We can be freed from blind control by vested interests. Alcoholics, with therapeutic help, can enter that lifelong phase called "recovering." Racism can yield to a society that actively asserts the worth of all.

We move now from the miracle story as such to the larger phenomenon of apocalyptic eschatology. Much of the literature written by the early church presupposes the apocalyptic way of thinking. At the surface level, the apocalyptic worldview poses great problems for intellectual and moral credibility. Relatively few people in the "mainline" churches today accept anything like a full-blown apocalyptic as a basis for understanding the world in which we live. Nor do many believe that history is literally divided into two disjunctive eras. Few expect Jesus to come riding on a cloud in order to intervene in a great historical cataclysm in which he will transform the world into a place of eternal delight in one single, violent event. We know that evil is real, but not many of us see it as the result of a literal Satan and demons. Apocalyptic thinking arose in communities whose social experience was that of marginality and oppression. The social world of most churchgoers is relatively comfortable and secure. Most American Christians are in a social position more like that of the dominant, oppressive forces that ancient apocalyptic theologians identified as embodying the old age! Few of us believe that history follows a predetermined script.

However, process interpreters find great positive value in aspects of apocalyptic eschatology. William A. Beardslee notices that the deeper intention of apocalyptic is to voice a radical openness to a new future for both individuals and the social and natural worlds in which we live. He notes that process thought "has been singularly aware of the requirement to be open to the new" and that this offers two possibilities for the reappropriation of apocalyptic texts. First, process thought "opens the way for a new grasp of infinity or totality as a religious concept." Not only is process theology cosmic in scope, unlike many contemporary theologies that seem not to know that God is related to nature, but it stresses that God offers new possibilities to emerging occasions. "Viewed this way, the infinite is, so to speak, separated into two parts: on the one hand, the infinity of possibility that offers an inexhaustible supply of the new, bit by bit, and on the other, God's infinite unification of experiences moment by moment. This way of being open to infinity or totality ceases to be threatening to the new and to hope."[33] Second, process thought affirms the possibility of human freedom that can be exercised freshly in every situation.

> Sociological conditions may indeed limit or even virtually exclude the effective exercise of freedom, but nevertheless it is a constant possibility—contrary to what many thinkers think today; thus, the "new" can be not only something we encounter but something to which we contribute. This conviction indeed can be powerfully liberating and can contribute to the actualization of possibilities of the exercise of freedom which otherwise would be ignored.[34]

Thus, while the surface witness of apocalyptic is problematic, its deeper witness is filled with promise when looked at from a process perspective.

The importance of theological analysis is clear as we extend our discussion to look at texts that raise different matters representative of difficult issues that preachers face throughout the Bible. At many points, process thought helps directly in reappropriating the text, while at others it allows the Christian community to distance itself from the witness of the text while retaining respect for the integrity of the text.

Joshua 6 recounts the defeat of Jericho as the people of Israel capture the promised land. Joshua declares that "the city and all that is within it shall be devoted to the LORD for destruction" (6:17). Obediently, the warriors "devoted to destruction by the edge of the sword all in the city, both men and women, young and old, oxen, sheep, and donkeys" (6:21). This text is only one of many that utilize the motif of the holy war. In this motif, God engages in warfare to accomplish God's holy will. The holy war comes about not simply as a result of the decisions of human political and military leaders but from the decision of God who acts in the role of divine warrior. In the church, we sometimes hear people assert that this "barbaric" picture of God is found only in the "Old Testament," that the "New Testament," by contrast, pictures a loving, gentle God. However, the motif of God as divine warrior is at the center of the apocalyptic theology that permeates the apostolic writings. Indeed, if anything, apocalyptic theology is more "barbaric" in its depiction of God, for the motif of God as divine warrior is projected to the cosmic scale. At the time of the second coming, Jesus acts as God's agent in fighting the cosmic battle.

The surface witness of Joshua 6 and many of the holy war texts is morally incredible. Where is God's love for the people of Jericho? But the motif of the holy war intends a deeper witness. God engages in holy war to be faithful to the promises that God made to Israel and (in Christian apocalyptic) to the church. The narrative thus calls the reader to trust in the God whose faithfulness is displayed in the victory won in the holy war. In the sermon, the preacher can criticize the theme of holy war as inappropriate to God's character and purposes while affirming the text's witness to God's faithfulness.

The parable of the wheat and the tares (Matt. 13:24–30, 36–43) raises the difficult issue of judgment. It depicts God as executing violent, negative judgment upon people because of their disobedience or unfaithfulness. God separates the wheat from the tares (the children of the realm of God from the children of the evil one) in a great judgment scene at the conclusion of the old age. The returning Jesus gathers up all the causes of sin and all the evildoers and throws them "into the furnace of fire, where there will be weeping and gnashing of teeth" (Matt. 13:42). In addition to the questions this text raises for the preacher by virtue of its being thoroughly apocalyptic, it forces the preacher to consider two particular questions. Are people—their motives, thoughts and behavior—so unambiguous that they can be neatly assigned to God or the devil? And where, in this parable, is the good news for those thrown into the pit of fire?

In this and similar texts, God is the agent (or authorizer) of acts of judgment that inflict savage consequences upon members of the human family. This is inappropriate to a gospel of unconditional love. Yet, at a deeper level, such texts can have instructive power. At the least, passages about judgment are a way of saying that our decisions, our actions, and values have consequences. Sometimes, these consequences are undesirable. A life that is lived as a tare can self-destruct. Whitehead argues that God provides for each finite occasion an initial aim at the highest relevant possibility for that occasion, that God offers to it the best aim that *can* be offered. What we become in life is the result of our freedom in responding or not responding to God's aims for us. We and God can arrive at a situation in which "the initial aim is the best for that *impasse*. But if the best be bad, then the ruthlessness of God can be personified as *Atè*, the goddess of mischief. The chaff is burnt."[35] A theological position that affirms both God's grace and our freedom must take our decisions seriously.

Furthermore, Russell Pregeant notes that the parable of the wheat and the tares functions as a fourfold lure. (1) At its heart, it lures us to recognize the two existential possibilities that "stand before the readers as church members." The text urges us to recognize the negative consequences of evil choices and to desire to make more positive choices. (2) It also urges readers to make a recommitment to Jesus and all that he represents in this gospel, and (3) to make a similar recommitment to God. (4) The text functions as a "universalistic lure toward recognition of God's primordial will which provides sanction for the confessional dimension."[36] Thus, while it is inappropriate to the gospel to say that God causes people to suffer, it is possible to find positive meaning in judgment passages.

Revelation 6:1–8 is a similar case. These verses contain the opening of the famous first four seals, "the four horses of the apocalypse." On a white horse a conquering rider carries a bow. On a red horse is a soldier. On a black horse is a rider carrying a balance and the vision is interpreted by a voice that describes a food shortage. On the fourth pale horse is death who kills with the sword, famine, pestilence, and wild beasts. These images, which seem rather strange to today's reader, would have been quite understandable to the first-century member of the church of the prophet John. The book of Revelation was written as an apocalyptic vision, using imagery drawn largely from the Hebrew Bible and other apocalyptic literature. John's purpose is not to lay out a road map of future events; it is to interpret the meaning of life from John's perspective in the Roman Empire.

This vision contributes to the purpose. The scroll on which the seven seals are placed is a symbol of understanding. The opening of the seals helps the reader grasp the meaning of certain aspects of life in imperial Rome. The first seal represents leadership in the empire that pretends to be of divine origin but is not, and is, therefore, idolatrous. The second is civil unrest and warfare. The third is a shortage of food, and the fourth is death. Such is life in the empire under Caesar, the rider on the white horse. The first-century reader would recognize behind these seals a Jewish understanding of the relationship between faithfulness to the covenant and subsequent conditions of blessing or curse. According to this way of thinking, exemplified especially in Deuteronomy and assumed by most prophets, those who are faithful to God are blessed while the unfaithful are cursed and need desperately to repent. The contents of the four seals are similar to the covenant curses described in Deuteronomy 28:15ff., thus indicating that John understands the situation in the Roman Empire to be one of curse. False leadership, violence, famine, and pestilence are visited upon Rome by God as a direct result of Rome's infidelity. The ultimate purpose of the curse is to cause Rome to repent. The curses are a kind of educational technique used by God to awaken human beings to their need to be faithful.

This text raises at least three important matters for the contemporary Christian preacher. One relates to the assumption underlying John's way of thinking. Is the relationship between blessing and curse so clearly a direct correlate of faithfulness? Plenty of people who appear to be unfaithful are prospering while some of the faithful are rotting away in conditions that seem to belong to the curse. Another issue has to do with the character of God. The text claims that God uses curses, such as civil unrest, famine, and death, for purposes of remedial education. Who is willing to stand before the hungry in Africa and tell them that their condition is given to them by God because they have been unfaithful and need to repent? That hardly sounds like a God whose nature is love and whose will is justice. Still another issue raised by this text is the relationship of nature to the divine will. According to John, the Deuteronomic editors and many other writers, nature is the direct agent of God which God uses to distribute blessing and curse. Today we do not speak of nature working in this way. Rather, we speak of natural elements working randomly without personal direction. Rain and tornadoes fall on the just and unjust alike. Theological analysis of the first two matters unfolds in much the same way as in the reflection on judgment. At the surface level, the relationship between the conditions of blessing and curse in community are not as simple as John believes. However, at a deeper level, such things as idolatry and the practice of injustice do lead to decay in a community. Our choices of whom to serve lead to conditions that we can recognize by the names "blessing" and "curse." Furthermore, at the surface level, we certainly would not say that God inflicts suffering on the world in order to cause it to repent. But, at a deeper level, we can regard the suffering and chaos of the world as a sign that it desperately needs the integrative vision and possibility that come only from God. Again, at the surface level, we today do not regard nature as the personal agent of God that, at God's behest, blesses some and curses others. But, at a deeper level, this text speaks to us (as does process theology) of the mutuality of humanity and nature. We are interdependent, as the ecological movement continuously reminds us. Nature, affected for good or ill by our decisions, can be a blessing or a curse; we can be a blessing or a curse to nature.

Clearly, then, theological evaluation is a most important step in moving from text to sermon. It helps define the relationship between today's community of faith and the text, and consequently, has a direct bearing on hermeneutics.

Meaning for Today

Hermeneutics is the critical discipline by which preachers move from the meaning of the text in its historical and literary setting to its meaning for the current congregation. When preaching from a biblical text, a common hermeneutical assumption is that the preacher is to *preach the text.* The preacher seeks for the biblical text to be the starting point and a controlling factor in the development of the sermon. An implicit supposition in such homiletical hermeneutics is that we can nearly always find a critical correlation between the text and today's world that will yield a positive meaning for the hearer. Thus, a criterion frequently employed in evaluation is: "Is the sermon true to the text?" Has the preacher properly understood the text and discovered a bridge from ancient to contemporary worlds that is consistent with the intention of the text?

However, *the purpose of the preacher is not to preach the text but is to preach the gospel.* When working from a biblical text, the preacher's purpose is to preach the gospel in the light of the text. When the text is appropriate to the gospel and credible, conventional hermeneutics works quite well. But when the text is inappropriate to the gospel, it hardly serves the gospel to preach the text. *Indeed, in this case, in order to preach the gospel one must preach against the text.* Here, the work of hermeneutics is to explain why the text is inappropriate or incredible and not authoritative for the church of today.

In the approach we have presented, two criteria are primary: theological appropriateness and credibility. While these are intimately related, they can at times function somewhat independently. It is, therefore, possible to see most texts as falling into one of the following categories:

1. Theologically appropriate and credible.
2. Theologically appropriate and incredible.
3. Theologically inappropriate and credible.
4. Theologically inappropriate and incredible.

This typology is complicated in actual practice by the complexity and individuality of particular texts. And it is further complicated by the difference between the surface meaning of a text and its deeper meaning.

In general, we may say that in the first case, the preacher agrees with the text. In the last case, the preacher fundamentally disagrees with the text. In the middle two options the preacher agrees with some aspects of the text but not others. Of course, the preacher might ignore a text.

a. *Agreement with the text.* The preacher can fundamentally agree with the witness of the text and can "preach the text." In this case the text is both theologically appropriate and credible. The witness of the text is consistent with the gospel and the cultural characteristics of the text do not pose an insuperable barrier to our appreciation of it. The preacher's task is to bring its claims into the consciousness of the hearers in a compelling way. Of course, some items found in the text may need to be explained for the benefit of the congregation, but when explained the witness of the text can be gladly received.

Genesis 28:10–17 is such a case. The stories of Genesis, given their present form around the time of the exile in Babylon, are understood by the editors as a mirror of the experience of Israel in every time and place. The story of Jacob is a part of the story of the whole community; Israel is similar to Jacob. Prior to Genesis 28:10–17, Jacob, true to the meaning of his name ("Grabber"), has conned the birthright and the blessing from his twin brother Esau and is fleeing to Haran in order to escape Esau's wrath. Now, on one night of his flight, he takes a rock for a pillow and lies down. As he sleeps, he dreams of a ladder that stretches from heaven to earth, upon which angels ascend and descend from the presence of God. God then speaks to Jacob. First, God reaffirms the promises of the land and descendants. Then, God says, "Know that I am with you and will keep you wherever you go, and will bring you back to this land; for I will not leave you until I have done what I have promised you" (Gen. 28:15).

The dream motif was a common device in the literature of Israel to authenticate an idea as divine in origin. The angels convey the awareness of God's providential presence. The climactic words from God indicate that a purpose of the text is to assure Jacob—and through his role in the text to assure the exiles—of the constancy of God's promises and God's presence. Although their behavior had taken them into exile, God was still with the exiles. This is welcome news. Just as God was faithful to the exiles in returning them to the land, so God is faithful to the promises God makes to all. The witness of this text is that God is faithful to the promises God has made to us and that God is with us, even though, like Jacob, we are thoroughly ambiguous. Jacob was justified by grace. So are we all.

The language of Psalm 147 is drawn from the creation narrative and the Sinai covenant. The psalm reveals that God's purpose is for all members of the community (nature included) to live in right relationship with one another and for every member to have access to the things that are necessary for a full life. A common biblical word for this condition in the community is "justice." However, the circumstances of some people left them on the margins of the community and perilously close to the edge of existence. In Psalm 147, these persons are represented by the oppressed, the hungry, the imprisoned, the blind, the bowed down, the sojourners, the widows, and the fatherless.

The psalm praises God because God is true to God's purposes for all. This is an essential element of God's reign. Thus, God executes justice for the oppressed and lifts up those who are bowed down. This is good news to the marginalized. As a hymn for the congregation, the psalm serves to remind leaders of the community of God's purpose for the whole community. When the leaders join the whole congregation in singing these words, they reaffirm their own willingness to lead the community in ordering itself justly. To those who today live on the edge of society, this psalm claims that the fundamental power of the universe wills for them to be lifted up. Psalm 147 reminds those who marginalize others that their own lives and communities will be full and whole only when all members are in right relationship with one another and with the resources of the community. Indeed, when the marginalizers become partners with God and with the sojourners, all are moved to say, "Praise the Lord."

Romans 8:31–39 is an archetypal example. Paul lists a series of life conditions and forces that could be taken to deny that God loves the community: the great judgment, tribulation, distress, persecution, famine, nakedness, peril, sword, angels, principalities, powers—items largely drawn from the thought-world of apocalypticism. Adherents of apocalyptic theology believed these things would be manifest in history in the years immediately prior to the apocalyptic cataclysm. Paul affirms that these conditions are not signs of God's displeasure or rejection. Rather, the unbreakable assurance of God's love, revealed in the death of Jesus, enables the community to survive the apocalyptic distress of tribulation, persecution, etc. Amid that distress, Christians become "more than conquerors."

We are not of the apocalyptic mind-set and do not believe in principalities and powers in the sense of personal devil-like beings. But the conditions described in the text are not tied inexplicably to the apocalyptic worldview and represent phenomena common to every era. While we may not believe in "principalities and powers" in the way that Paul did, we do experience transpersonal forces in the world through such forms as systemic evil and the arbitrary, brutal exercise of power by those in positions of authority. Much in the world in the late twentieth century can be described by these conditions. In this setting, the text speaks an appropriate and intelligible word: God's love permeates *every* situation in which our world finds itself.

While actual circumstances of difficulty may not change, the awareness of God's love can transform our perspective on it such that it does not "conquer" us but, instead, becomes the occasion for a potent witness. The cancer patient may not get well, but even in the midst of dying can become aware of God's presence. Indeed, the way in which Christians die can be a powerful witness. A victim of racial injustice may find that the awareness of God's unconditional evaluation of the person as a person of worth may be precisely what enables that person to rise up and challenge the system of injustice.

Ephesians 2:1–10 starkly describes the situation of Gentiles before the appearance of the grace of God to them in Jesus Christ. "You were dead through the trespasses and sins in which you once lived, following the course of this world, following the ruler of the power of the air, the spirit that is now at work among those who are disobedient. All of us once lived among them in the passions of our flesh, following the desires of flesh and senses, and we were by nature children of wrath, like everyone else" (2:1–3). This Gentile existence is the functional equivalent of death. But now, Gentiles have been made *alive* through the grace of God (2:1, 5, 8).

Henceforth, Gentiles accept God's grace as the all-sufficient basis for their self-understanding, and commit themselves to lives of witness for God. This is salvation.

The marvel, according to Ephesians, is God's *grace*, God's unmerited favor upon those (Gentiles) who least deserve it. The Gentiles have been enemies of God but now, apart from any achievement on their part, God makes them alive. This passage still warms the hearts of Christians. For most of us are Gentiles and would have no acquaintance with God were it not for the revelation of God's mercy and love in Jesus Christ. In an achievement-oriented culture that counts human worth on the basis of performance, we are freed from trying to prove our worth to God and one another. As a hymn says, "*Nothing* in my hand I bring, simply to thy cross I cling."[37]

b. *Agreement with parts of the text and disagreement with other parts.* This mixed evaluation may well be the most frequent result of evaluating texts. Often the preacher will find that a text contains an appropriate theological affirmation expressed in a worldview that is no longer credible. In other passages, the worldview expressed in the passage may not be troubling but the theological premise may be offensive. The situation may be further complicated when the preacher considers the surface and deeper levels of the text. At the former, the text may be objectionable from the point of view of either theological appropriateness or credibility, but the deeper meaning may be more promising.

As we have seen, Mark 1:21–28 presumes a surface worldview to which we no longer adhere. But beneath this cultural expression is a still-potent theological affirmation. Any number of miracle stories in the Bible fall into this pattern, from the crossing of the Red Sea (Exodus 3:17—14:31), to the ever-filling cruse of oil at Zarephath (1 Kings 17:8–16), to the three children in the fiery furnace (Daniel 3:1–30), to Jesus' feedings of the thousands. When dealing with such texts, it is incumbent upon preachers to explain why the claim of the text is believable despite its expression in a strange worldview.

Psalm 75 illustrates a case in which the same text manifests theologically appropriate and inappropriate elements, as well as elements which are intelligible and unintelligible. On the one hand, it is appropriate to see God as one who steadies the earth in the threat of chaos (75:3), but not appropriate that God would pour a cup of foaming poison for the enemy (75:8). It is not, on the surface, intelligible to see the earth as a platform set on pillars, but it is certainly intelligible to think of the congregation singing praise (75:1a) because of its awareness of God's presence amidst the chaos of the world.

Most texts in the Gospel of John fall into a pattern found in many other parts of the apostolic writings. In John, the text often contains an affirmation of the gospel made at the expense of others. The Fourth Gospel will often claim that the gracious love of God is operative for Christians but will deny it to others, especially Jews. The theological affirmation at the heart of the text is both appropriate and inappropriate. John 3:16–21 begins with one of the most famous and well-loved texts in the Bible. It claims that God loves *the world* and gave Jesus that all who believe in him will not perish but have everlasting life. This is appropriate to the gospel, credible and true to the experience of the church. But this text also asserts that all who do not become Christian are already condemned, rejected by God (3:18). These latter love the darkness, the domain of the devil, because they themselves are evil and hate the light. In John, the nonbelievers are primarily Jews and no longer recipients of God's love; they are children of the devil (8:12–59). This is inappropriate to the gospel. Indeed, John 3:16 stands in judgment on the attitude voiced in John 3:18. The preacher then can agree with and preach part of the text—God's love for the world and the definitive revelation of that love through Jesus. But the preacher can only preach against the claim that God rejects all those—especially Jews—who do not become Christian.

A text will sometimes make a statement based on a historical inaccuracy. In some instances the inaccuracy is intentional and serves a theological purpose. The most concentrated number of examples of this phenomenon is in the gospels in which the Jewish people, especially the Pharisees, are consistently and grossly misrepresented.[38] Our understanding of Jewish religious life, particularly of Pharisaism, has been radically revised in the last generation. Where once we regarded first-century Jewish religious life as stagnated, legalistic, and preoccupied with ceremony and outward show, we now see it as vibrant, alive, and centered in a gracious God. Pharisees were concerned with practicing the mercy and justice of God in everyday affairs. The caricature of Judaism that appears in the narratives of the gospels is the result of intense antagonism between the church and synagogue between about 65 and 100 C.E. when the gospel stories were given their present forms. When we repeat the caricature even for the purpose of making an analogy with the contemporary congregation ("Friends, our prayers this morning are like those of the ancient Pharisees...") we contribute subtly to anti-Judaism.

A clear representative of this phenomenon is Matthew 6:1–6, 16–21, which provides an anti-Pharisaic context for the Lord's Prayer and accuses Pharisees of giving alms only for the sake of human praise, of praying in public to be seen by other people, and of fasting with public display of disfigurement to receive other people's admiration. However, according to the Pharisees' self-description, these are acts of genuine piety and devotion. To represent the Pharisees in bald, negative fashion is inaccurate; it is morally implausible for those of us who are commanded not to bear false witness against our neighbors. Therefore, preachers should correct such historical misunderstandings in the name of the gospel's proclamation of God's love for each and all and God's command that justice be done to each and all. We can learn to practice the hermeneutic of suspicion on the "historical data" in a text. Data that are particularly open to scrutiny are the portrayal of the enemies of Israel, Jesus or the church. When such data are found to be false, and especially when used polemically, we should employ a "hermeneutic of correction."

c. *Ignoring of the text.* The preacher can always, intentionally or unintentionally, ignore a text and never preach on it. In churches that do not use a lectionary and leave selection of preaching texts entirely to the preacher, a text will be ignored because it neither catches the preacher's attention nor falls into the preacher's range of concerns; perhaps its import is difficult to grasp, or its point runs counter to the preacher's theology. Whatever the reason for ignoring a text, the result is the same: The congregation is never exposed to the text in public worship, and many members are never exposed to it at all.

The same thing happens in churches that use a lectionary. Preachers who regularly follow a lectionary often comment appreciatively that it prevents them from turning repeatedly to the same texts and that the lections force preachers into parts of the Bible where they would not otherwise go. A frequent comment is, "The lectionary really made me wrestle with that text." This is all to the good, since lectionaries contain a broad sweep of material from the Bible. But lectionaries also encourage ministers to overlook texts. This happens in two ways. For one, the number of texts in a lectionary is small when compared to the corpus of the Bible itself. The Common Lectionary provides for only about 600 readings (not counting Psalms) over a three-year period.[39] Of these, only about 160 are from the Hebrew Bible (a little more than 25 percent), even though the Hebrew Bible is 80 percent of the canon. For another, texts that are included in lectionaries are not always broadly representative of the fabric of the Bible. Of the 600 readings in the Common Lectionary, about 75 appear (in whole or in part) more than once. The number of passages is diminished further by the fact that parallel passages from the synoptic gospels often appear in years A, B and C. Of the 150 Psalms, selections from 114 are designated for use and, of these, 58 are at least partly repeated on different Sundays.

Beyond the limitation on the number of texts in the lectionary is the types of texts that are underrepresented or missing altogether. The fact that only 25 percent of the total lectionary readings are from the Hebrew Bible devalues the importance of that literature for the church and quietly reinforces the unfortunate Christian devaluation of Judaism and Jews. This augments Christian ignorance concerning Jewish history, belief and practice and thereby detracts from Christian acquaintance with the background of our own history, beliefs and practices.

Again, despite the prominence and frequency of passages, especially in the prophetic books, which highlight the importance of justice in the life of the community, relatively few appear in the lectionaries. This gives concern for justice a relatively low profile in the mind of the listener whose primary source about the Bible is the Sunday service. Indeed, modern lectionaries are criticized for reflecting the theological, social and economic biases of their largely white, middle-class, bureaucratically entrenched compilers. The hermeneutic of suspicion can be applied to the lectionaries in common use today.[40]

Despite the praise heaped upon lectionaries for helping preachers and congregations engage difficult texts, the lectionaries avoid the most difficult texts. Representative of those that are not included in the Common Lectionary, and whose qualities are not such as to make them magnets for preachers who select their own preaching texts, are the following:

- Numbers 16–17: The revolt of Korah comes to an end when God despises Korah, splits asunder the ground under Korah and his followers and swallows them all.

- Judges 4:17–22: Jael drives a tent peg through the head of Sisera.

- 1 Samuel 28: Saul consults the spirit of the dead Samuel by means of a medium at Endor.

- Psalm 109: The psalmist prays for the prayer of the enemy to be counted as sin, for the days of the enemy to be few and the enemy's children orphaned and beggars, for the enemy to lose every worldly possession, and for the curse of the Lord to become the clothing of the enemy.

- Mark 4:10–12: Through a passage from Isaiah that is put into the mouth of Jesus, Mark states that God has caused many people not to understand the parables, the ministry of Jesus or the dawning rule of God.

- John 8:12–59: The Johannine Jesus identifies the Jews as children of the devil.

- Acts 5:1–10: Ananias and Sapphira drop dead because they lie to Peter.

- 1 Corinthians 15:29–33: Paul appears to approve of the Corinthian practice of living persons being baptized as proxies on behalf of the dead.

- Colossians 3:18—4:1, Ephesians 5:21—6:9, 1 Peter 2:11—3:7: "Household codes" prescribe a hierarchy of authority in society and home that include the relationship of people to the state and the relationship of men and women, and assume the validity of slavery.

- Revelation 16:1–21: God commands an angel to pour seven bowls of wrath upon the earth for the purpose of causing humanity to repent.

To one degree or another, all these texts are inappropriate to the gospel. Given the rejection, violence and death inflicted in these texts, it is no wonder that they, and others like them, are ignored. However, to ignore such texts is to risk giving the impression that their witness is acceptable to the Christian community. As long as these texts are left uninterpreted by the community, individual members are left to interpret them on the basis of their own idiosyncrasies and often arbitrary and self-serving purposes.

Furthermore, *to ignore such texts is to miss an important teaching opportunity.* A hermeneutical task of the preacher is to help the congregation understand the relationship of the text to the Christian witness. If the text is inappropriate or incredible, this needs to be stated and explained. At the same time, the preacher not only teaches the congregation about a specific text but models a theological method that the members can then employ on other texts and use in evaluating extra-biblical texts, ideas, relationships, and situations. Preachers may find it helpful to preach sermons that review the sources and content of the gospel message and show how to use that message in the analysis of tradition and of contemporary life.

Preachers should welcome the opportunity to take the most difficult text as a starting point for the sermon. To do so is to exercise one of the fundamental roles of leadership in the Christian community, that of teacher of the Christian faith. The teacher does not hide from the tradition, even its most puzzling and difficult parts, but interprets it for the benefit of all.

d. *Disagreement with the text.* When the text is altogether inappropriate to the gospel, and incredible, the preacher may employ a hermeneutic of disagreement. In this case the hermeneutical work of the preacher is to show why the theological claims of the text are inappropriate to the gospel and/or why the text is not otherwise credible. The minister preaches the gospel against the text. We hasten to note four things. First, there will be few times for altogether dismissing the witness of a text. When we use the distinction between the surface and deeper witness of a text, we can usually find some positive point of contact between the text and the situation of today's listeners. Second, the difficulties posed by some few texts seem to call for fundamental disagreement with them, even though the texts themselves may have at least a thread of positive value at the level of their deeper witness. Third, we always regard the text respectfully. We cannot be true to the gospel or to process thought by playing fast and loose with a text. Often when we disagree with a text, we do so reluctantly and painfully. Fourth, the occasion of preaching against the text needs to be an occasion for encountering the gospel. The text itself may not channel the gospel to the church, but the preacher can remind the congregation of the fundamental convictions of the gospel in the process of dealing with the text and its problems.

In Psalm 137, for example, after a poignant lament over the fall of Jerusalem and the community's exile in Babylon in verses 1–6, the psalm comes to this climax in the form of a prayer:

> Remember, O LORD, against the Edomites
>   the day of Jerusalem's fall,
> how they said, "Tear it down! Tear it down!
>   Down to its foundations!"
> O daughter Babylon, you devastator!
>   Happy shall they be who pay you back
>   what you have done to us!
> Happy shall they be who take your little ones
>   and dash them against the rock!
> Psalm 137:7–9

The psalmist here advocates that vengeance be done to the enemies of Israel. Indeed, the agent of vengeance will be *happy* to dash the babies of the Babylonians against the rock. This text contradicts the heart of the gospel message, as of the Hebrew scriptures' understanding of the singular love and justice of God.

In 2 Kings 2:23–25, the prophet Elisha is walking to Bethel when some small boys jeer at him. Elisha curses them and immediately two bears come from the woods and tear up forty-two of the boys. This monstrous act is attributed to a prophet of the Lord. Jeremiah 13:1–13 quotes God as punishing the people by causing them to perish by the sword and their dead to be as dung. God takes peace away from the people so that there is no comfort even for those who mourn. God hurls them out of the land and delivers them to other gods. God withdraws the divine "steadfast love and mercy." Such behavior hardly manifests "steadfast love."

First Peter 2:13—3:7 assumes a view of the universe as a hierarchy with God at the top and each subsequent authority having power over a specific area of responsibility. Under ordinary conditions, those under a power were expected to obey it. At the heart of this model, adapted from the Hellenistic milieu, is the idea that God prevents chaos in the world by establishing hierarchical order. Thus, this text exhorts its readers to obey the emperor and his representatives and to regard the emperor as an agent of God (2:13–17). Slaves are admonished to be submissive to their masters, even to the point of enduring pain (2:18–25). Wives are to be submissive to their husbands and the dress of the wife is prescribed. Sarah, who appears here as the archetypal wife, addressed her husband (Abraham) as "Lord" (3:1–6). Husbands are encouraged to live considerately with their wives since the latter are the weaker sex (3:7).

The passage is full of problems. In concert with virtually all of the Bible, it assumes the validity of slavery. This kind of passage has been used to justify human slavery. This is chilling. This passage assumes absolute loyalty to the ruling government. Many church leaders follow John Calvin in arguing that the authority of political leaders is valid only as long as they act in accordance with the purposes of God.[41] Further, the passage assumes the validity of a monarchical form of government not directly responsive to or responsible for the people. Absolute loyalty to government at any level is hardly an unquestioned mark of faithfulness. The relationship between husbands and wives is here described in strictly hierarchical terms. Some interpreters have attempted to explain the word "submissive," to take away some of its sting. The companion part of the passage does require the husband to be considerate of the wife. But, the hierarchy cannot be explained away and the call to consideration is still in the context of hierarchy. This passage and others similar to it have been used to justify acts of abuse that range from the psychological to the physical. The egalitarian thrust of the gospel is in direct opposition to the viewpoint of this text.

In this passage, the relationship between God's love for all and the assumptions of the pericope is tested. How can one believe that God loves another person and then enslave that person? How can one automatically assume that a particular act of government—like capital punishment—is consistent with the gospel? How does the appeal to the submission of one human being to another on the basis of marital status and gender say to the woman, "God loves you with gracious love?" How does that say: "God calls for justice for you"? What is inherent in being male that should cause males to be regarded as superior?

This text has a deeper witness. In the light of the worldview in which it was written, it calls for all things to live in their proper relationship so as to stave off personal and social chaos. We today think not of hierarchicalism but of egalitarianism and mutuality as staving off personal and social chaos. But the text itself, and others like it, has led to so much human oppression that it is difficult to imagine that it can be reclaimed in our time. Here process hermeneutics offers a glimmer of hope. For while the text seems not to speak a strong word to the present, conceivably in another cultural milieu it could be reappropriated so as to overcome the problems of its past and offer some presently unrecognized possibility to the world.

As we have noted, at the surface level a text may use an image that is inappropriate to the gospel but that, at the deeper level, can be understood to have a positive meaning. However, the preacher should be cautious in using the text in a positive way if the surface image seems to sanction brutality or oppression or to misrepresent God in a fundamental way. Even though one may explain the text very carefully, the listeners are still left with a warped image to function in an authoritative way in the church. Recent studies have discovered that images play a crucial role in the consciousness of the listener in forming the listener's perception of the world and God and in shaping the listener's behavior.[42] The images planted in our minds tend to pattern our thoughts and actions. Therefore, the preacher may not wish to leave an inappropriate image in the mind of the congregation, for that image may remain longer than its interpretation and even unconsciously work against the interpretation given to it.

The story of the death of Uzzah in 2 Samuel 6:1–15 is such a case. Uzzah was helping to bring the ark of the covenant to Jerusalem when the oxen pulling the ark stumbled and the ark began to ride precariously. Uzzah touched the ark to steady it, and "the anger of the Lord was kindled against Uzzah; and God struck him there because he reached out his hand to the ark; and he died there beside the ark of God" (6:7). On the surface this text is neither appropriate nor intelligible. What kind of God would destroy a person for trying to prevent damage to the ark? And how would God be able to act in the world so as to cause Uzzah to die on the spot?

Still, Thomas G. Long has argued that a positive meaning for this and other texts can be recovered by paying attention to the function of the text. In this case, the text appears as part of a larger "ark narrative" that traces the progress of the ark to Jerusalem and underlines God's initiative while downplaying the human role in this progress. Uzzah, according to Long, "represents all human effort to manipulate the divine presence and favor," where the ark itself "symbolizes the power and presence of God above human control." Hence, "the story celebrates the triumph of the 'ark' symbol over the 'Uzzah' symbol." The sermon, then, "must present the same symbols in contemporary terms and develop the same tension as does the original."[43]

This brilliant effort, however, still leaves the reader/listener with an image of God that is inappropriate to the gospel. A God of unconditional love would not kill a human being for trying to help God's purposes. A God who causes Uzzah to die on the spot is not a God of unconditional love. After reading this story are we not forever afraid of violating the conditionality of Uzzah's God? The kind of sovereignty pictured in this text has the effect of undermining trust in the very God to whom the text is a witness. Until the wrong-headedness of the text is challenged, listeners are left with an image that misrepresents God, God's action in the world, and the human response to God.

A pastoral note is in order here. Public and plainspoken disagreement with the Bible is something to which many congregations are unaccustomed. While such a tack will prove a great relief to some listeners, others initially will be deeply troubled by it and some may even think it unchristian. Therefore, for reasons both intrinsic to the gospel and of pedagogical strategy, the preacher may be well advised not to run roughshod over the text or the congregation. Since the gospel is the news of God's unmerited and unconditional love for all, the preacher's homiletical strategy should be consistent with that love and should treat the text and the hearers with sensitivity, care, and respect. To be sure, the preacher's calling is to tell the truth; sometimes the truth is painful, but this is all the more reason to be positive and gentle while being straightforward.

The preacher's homiletical strategy will be well served by this attitude as well. A study of learning patterns shows that persons tend to become defensive and resistant when confronted in a high-handed, belittling manner. The optimum environment for a change of thinking is one in which learners feel valued by and in community with other learners and especially the leader.[44] Of particular value in effecting a change in thinking is the leader's own story and rationale. Students and congregants tend to regard this story as a model to follow in the risk of letting go of the familiar and entertaining the new. It may prove helpful for preachers to acknowledge their initial reservations about disagreeing with a text and to rehearse those ideas and experiences that contributed to the formation of the new consciousness.

Strange as it may sound, liberation is often a painful process even for those who are most oppressed. The condition of oppression offers the security of the familiar where liberation is fraught with the terror that often accompanies the unknown. Encouragement in the transition is crucial and can be effectively provided by the pastor who is trusted, sensitive, careful, imaginative, and honest. Therefore, preaching against the text may well be the preacher's most challenging homiletical assignment and call forth one's best and most creative effort.

Thus, the prerequisites for the preacher are a critical understanding of the gospel, an intelligent understanding of the contemporary situation, and moral sensitivity. Preachers who are so informed can engage the Bible in preaching in the confidence that Christian witness will result.

Notes

[1]David J. Lull, "What Is Process Hermeneutics?", *Process Studies*, Vol. 13 (1974), p. 192. William A. Beardslee, et al., make the same point in *Biblical Preaching on the Death of Jesus*, p. 41.

[2]J. Gerald Janzen notes that "at the heart of process there is a basic conceptuality, and a central imagery of such suggestive power and so elucidatory of the world and human experience, that its application to biblical theology would contribute greatly to the deeper grasp of the biblical witness, in modes of thought which would at once be faithful to its historic meaning and expressive of its contemporary 'cash value.'" ("The Old Testament in 'Process' Perspective: Proposal for a Way Forward in Biblical Theology," in Frank

Moore Cross, Werner E. Lemke, and Patrick D. Miller, Jr., eds., *Magnalia Dei* [Garden City: Doubleday, 1976], p. 507.) Janzen and other writers are careful to warn us against construing the biblical writers as process thinkers. While there are points of similarity between biblical and process modes of thought, the particular value of process conceptuality is to give us a philosophical framework that can help explain, extend, develop, and reinterpret the insights of the Bible. For further illustrations of this approach, see William A. Beardslee, *A House for Hope* (Philadelphia: Westminster Press, 1972); Neill Q. Hamilton, *Jesus For a No-God World* (Philadelphia: Westminster Press, 1969); *Journal of the American Academy of Religion*, Vol. 47, No. 1 (1979); *Semeia*, Vol. 24 (1982); and David J. Lull, *The Spirit in Galatia*, SBL Dissertation Series (Chico: Scholars Press, 1980).

[3]While it is beyond the purpose of this chapter to offer a systematic construction of ways in which a process perspective can illuminate the interpretation of the broad range of biblical texts, we do point out that the theme of the divine lure is one of the most frequently used motifs in process biblical interpretation. Process interpreters often see a text as a lure for feeling. That is, the text is an attempt to lure readers into understanding themselves differently or acting differently. This is especially helpful when we encounter texts that depict God as acting in ways that are morally difficult. The text itself may contain morally problematic material, but the occasion of considering the text can be positive as we recognize that its function is to lure the reader into making wise choices that say "yes" to God's future. See, e.g., Lewis S. Ford, *The Lure of God* (Philadelphia: Fortress Press, 1978).

[4]On conversation as a model for understanding our relationship with texts, see David Tracy, *Plurality and Ambiguity* (San Francisco: Harper & Row, 1987), pp. 1-28.

[5]E.g., Paul Ricoeur, *Freud and Philosophy*, tr. Denis Savage (New Haven: Yale University Press, 1970).

[6]Lull, "What Is Process Hermeneutics?", claims that "Scripture is not necessary, however important it is, in and for Christian faith and life" (p. 197).

[7]Paul Ricoeur, *Interpretation Theory* (Fort Worth: Texas Christian University Press, 1974), pp. 45-56.

[8]Norman Perrin and David Duling, *The New Testament: An Introduction*, rev. ed. (New York: Harcourt, Brace, Jovanovich, 1982), p. 233.

[9]This account of apocalyptic theology is quite general. Many apocalyptic documents differ at some points.

[10]This text initiates a most unfortunate theme that develops throughout the narrative and reaches its focal point in the stories of the trial and crucifixion of Jesus: namely, that the Jewish people are themselves possessed (14:10-11, 43ff.). For heuristic purposes we do not deal with these and other larger matters but focus on the single pericope. See further Clark M. Williamson and

Ronald J. Allen, *Interpreting Difficult Texts* (London: SCM, and Philadelphia: Trinity Press International, 1989), pp. 40-42.

[11]Antoinette C. Wire, "The Structure of the Gospel Miracle Stories and Their Tellers," *Semeia*, Vol. 11 (1978), p. 109.

[12]David G. Buttrick, "Interpretation and Preaching," *Interpretation*, Vol. 24 (1981), p. 52; *Homiletic* (Philadelphia: Fortress Press, 1987), p. 268f.

[13]As we noted in the previous chapter, it is sometimes possible to criticize the surface witness of the text on the basis of a deeper witness. It is also possible to criticize the witness of a specific pericope on the basis of the witness of the larger document in which the specific passage is found, and on the basis of the scriptures' own self-correcting hermeneutic.

[14]This interpretation is long-standing and deep-seated, at least at the popular level. Note, e.g., Lynn White, "The Historical Roots of Our Ecological Crisis," *Science*, Vol. 155 (1967), pp. 1203-1207. Elaine Pagels chronicles the uses made of this story in the early centuries of the church in her *Adam, Eve and the Spirit* (New York: Random House, 1988).

[15]Genesis 1, with its provision that Adam and Eve and the animals could have only plants for food (vs. 29-30), is clearly aware of the moral-ethical complexities involved in killing food. Process thought, too, has known that "life is robbery. It is at the point that with life morals become acute. The robber requires justification." Alfred North Whitehead, *Process and Reality* (Corrected Edition), p. 105. See also Daniel A. Dombrowski, *Hartshorne and the Metaphysics of Animal Rights* (Albany: State University of New York Press, 1988).

[16]For an example of a re-reading of this text, see Walter Brueggemann, *Genesis*, Interpretation Commentary (Atlanta: John Knox Press, 1982), p. 32f.

[17]Phyllis Trible, *God and the Rhetoric of Sexuality* (Philadelphia: Fortress Press, 1978), p. 173.

[18]*Ibid.*, p. 195.

[19]The guild of scholars has not established a consensus on a revised picture of Paul, but the general mood of current scholarship is to see Paul in considerably more sympathy with his Jewish roots than in earlier generations.

[20]Lloyd Gaston, *Paul and the Torah* (Vancouver: University of British Columbia Press, 1987), p. 68.

[21]*Ibid.*, p. 69f.

[22]*Ibid.*, p. 106.

[23]*Ibid.*, p. 76ff.

[24]*Ibid.*, p. 72ff.

[25]Throughout this book we have been speaking of three norms in Christian theology (appropriateness to the gospel, intellectual credibility and moral credibility). Here, we speak of only two: appropriateness and credibility. For purposes of simplification, especially in the next subsection, "Meaning for

Today," we have brought intelligibility and moral plausibility into one rubric (credibility). As we argued in the previous chapter, these criteria are distinguishable but inseparable.

²⁶These are discussed further by Schubert M. Ogden in *The Point of Christology* (San Francisco: Harper & Row, 1982), pp. 89-96; *On Theology* (New York: Harper & Row, 1986), pp. 4-6; and "The Service of Theology to the Servant Task of Ministry," in E. Earl Shelp and Ronald D. Sunderland, eds., *The Pastor as Servant* (New York: Pilgrim, 1986), pp. 87-93. Cf. David Tracy, *Blessed Rage for Order* (New York: Seabury, 1975), pp. 72-81; *The Analogical Imagination* (New York: Crossroad, 1981), pp. 59, 238-240; and Tracy, with Robert M. Grant, *A Short History of the Interpretation of the Bible* (Philadelphia: Fortress Press, 1984), pp. 174-176.

²⁷Beardslee *et al.*, *Biblical Preaching on the Death of Jesus*, p. 47.

²⁸The text does make a derisive comment concerning the scribes who, in contrast to Jesus, did not teach with authority. In the larger context of the narrative, Mark implies that the Jews are possessed by demons and have rejected God because they rejected Jesus. As a consequence, their temple is destroyed (15:38) and their house falls (3:20–27). Mark's God does not love each and every Jew.

²⁹Wire, "The Structure of the Gospel Miracle Stories and Their Tellers," p. 109.

³⁰Walter Wink, *Naming the Powers* (Philadelphia: Fortress Press, 1984), p. 5. Cf. Wink, *Unmasking the Powers* (Philadelphia: Fortress Press, 1986), esp. pp. 41-68, "The Demons."

³¹Neill Q. Hamilton identifies representative "social equivalents of possession" today: the work demon, the consumer demon, the sex demon. *The Recovery of the Protestant Adventure* (New York: Seabury, 1981), p. 71ff.

³²On the image of Christ functioning in this way, see Beardslee, *A House for Hope*, pp. 150-174.

³³William A. Beardslee, "Openness to the New in Apocalyptic and in Process Theology," *Process Studies*, Vol. 3 (1973), p. 176. This is a favorite theme of process biblical interpreters, e.g., Beardslee, *A House for Hope*, pp. 96-149; Lewis Ford, *The Lure of God,* pp. 113-121; Russell Pregeant, *Mystery Without Magic* (Oak Park, IL: Meyer-Stone, 1988), pp. 160-176; Beardslee, *et al.*, *Biblical Preaching on the Death of Jesus*, p. 45f.

³⁴Beardslee, "Openness to the New in Apocalyptic and in Process Theology," p. 177.

³⁵Whitehead, *Process and Reality* (Corrected Edition), p. 244.

³⁶Russell Pregeant, *Christology Beyond Dogma*, SBL Semeia Supplements (Missoula: Scholars Press, 1978), p. 125f. On judgment, cf. Janzen, "The Old Testament in Process Perspective," p. 502f. Reinhold Niebuhr finds that the parable encourages us to be patient with the ambiguities of history in

his *Moral Man and Immoral Society* (New York: Charles Scribner's Sons, 1932), pp. 209-213.

[37] Augustus Toplady, "Rock of Ages," in *The Hymnal* (Philadelphia: Presbyterian Board of Christian Education, 1938), p. 237.

[38] This problem is considered in detail in Williamson and Allen, *Interpreting Difficult Texts*, pp. 28-55.

[39] *The Common Lectionary* (New York: The Church Hymnal Corporation, 1983).

[40] For evaluations of the lectionary approach to preaching, see Catherine and Justo Gonzalez, *Liberation Preaching* (Nashville: Abingdon Press, 1980), pp. 38-47; William Skudlarek, *The Word in Worship* (Nashville: Abingdon Press, 1981), pp. 45-64; James A. Sanders, "Canon and Calendar," in Dieter T. Hessel, ed., *Social Themes of the Christian Year* (Philadelphia: Geneva, 1983), pp. 257-263; Lloyd Bailey, "The Lectionary in Critical Perspective," *Interpretation*, Vol. 31 (1977), pp. 139-153; Peter Bower, *Handbook for the Common Lectionary* (Philadelphia: Geneva, 1987), pp. 15-30; Williamson and Allen, *Interpreting Difficult Texts*, pp. 112-115.

[41] John Calvin, *Institutes of the Christian Religion*, ed. John T. MeNeill, tr. Ford L. Battles (Philadelphia: Westminster Press, 1950), p. 1520.

[42] E.g., George Lakhoff and Mark Johnson, *Metaphors We Live By* (Chicago: University of Chicago Press, 1980), p. 3ff.; Kenneth Boulding, *The Image* (Ann Arbor: University of Michigan Press, 1956); Dwight Bolingen, *Language: The Loaded Weapon* (New York: Longmans, 1980). Note especially David G. Buttrick, *Homiletic* (Philadelphia: Fortress Press, 1987), *passim*.

[43] Thomas G. Long, "The Fall of the House of Uzzah and Other Difficult Preaching Texts," *Journal for Preachers*, Vol. 7 (1983), p. 16. For Long's fully developed consideration of the hermeneutical value of paying attention to the function of texts, see his *Preaching and the Literary Forms of the Bible* (Philadelphia: Fortress Press, 1989).

[44] D. Bruce Roberts, "Theological Education and Field Education: A Parallel Process," lecture at Christian Theological Seminary, 1988.

Chapter

Sermons from a
Process Perspective

The test of a homiletical theory is in the preaching that flows from that theory. Does a theory yield sermons that are appropriate to the gospel, credible and morally plausible?[1] Does it generate sermons that shine a ray of hope on the daily paths of the listeners? Does it bring forth sermons that help the congregation make sense, in the light of the gospel, out of the full range of life's experiences? Does it provide practical moral guidance for the moment-to-moment decisions that we all must make? Does a homiletical theory encourage sermons that engage the full range of human sources of knowledge, that is, does the sermon evoke feeling? Does the theory give rise to sermons that are interesting and does it honor the freedom of the listeners? Most importantly, does the homiletical theory help the community become conscious of and responsive to the redemptive presence of the living God in their daily living? We believe that preaching from the perspective of process theology can yield such sermons.[2]

In this chapter, we offer two sermons that illustrate process principles in preaching. The sermons are somewhat different in style and approach, as are the individuals who preached them. We do not print these sermons as ideals to be emulated. Indeed, process thinking calls for preachers to develop their own voices as befits novel individuals. Rather, we hope that these sermons illustrate that process thought is a practical help for the preparation of sermons that can be preached in a typical congregation.[3] The preacher can translate process conceptuality into everyday English that can be understood and appreciated by shopkeepers, schoolteachers, maintenance workers, physicians, and youth full of wide-eyed wonder.

We provide a brief introduction to each sermon that orients the reader to the salient considerations in its development. We have left time-dated references in the sermons.

On Cutting Off Your Hand[4]

Text: "Whoever causes one of these little ones who believe in me to sin, it would be better for him if a great millstone were hung round his neck and he were thrown into the sea. And if your hand causes you to sin, cut it off; it is better for you to enter life maimed than with two hands to go to hell, to the unquenchable fire. And if your foot causes you to sin, cut it off; it is better for you to enter life lame than with two feet to be thrown into hell. And if your eye causes you to sin, pluck it out; it is better for you to enter the kingdom of God with one eye than with two eyes to be thrown into hell, where their worm does not die, and the fire is not quenched. For every one will be salted with fire. Salt is good; but if the salt has lost its saltness, how will you season it? Have salt in yourselves, and be at peace with one another."

Mark 9:42–50, RSV

Orientation: This sermon was prompted by the appearance of the text in The Common Lectionary. On the surface, the text is exceptionally problematic. It seems to be neither appropriate to the gospel, nor plausible either intellectually or morally. Using the methodology outlined in the preceding chapter, I determined through exegesis that even in the worldview of Mark, the text did not call for people to mutilate themselves physically. The text is, rather, an example of graphic hyperbole. In visceral imagery, it calls for the listeners to embrace the rule of God with the whole of their lives. In essence, the text says: "Hold nothing back!" Thus, the text does make a deeper point of positive value. We can, in this way, partially agree with the text and partially disagree with it.

I take the text as a lure that intends to draw people to God and to the possibilities for the future that are offered through the image of the rule of God. In the sermon itself, I first attempt to deal with questions that the text is likely to raise in the minds of listeners, e.g., "Should we take this text literally?" The text is then placed in the context of the larger Markan worldview. I briefly outline points of similarity and dissimilarity between Mark's worldview and our world and show that, despite differences, there are points at which the text is instructive for us. Finally, the sermon moves to offer images that are intended to evoke a feeling of love for God and a desire to say "Yes" to God. I hope to displace the negative imagery of the text with imagery that is more positive and appropriate.

The Sermon

As a professor of preaching, I have two fundamental convictions regarding Christian preaching. First, Christian preaching is basically good news from God that renews the life of the world. Second, Christian preaching is basically indicative: It tells us what God has done and continues to do for you and me and for everything in this crazy world. Indicative preaching is in contrast to imperative preaching in which the preacher tries to tell the congregation what *they* should *do*.

Few passages in the Bible run more against the grain of my convictions than the one we just heard from the Gospel of Mark. This text is imperative from beginning to end. There are only 150 words in the whole passage and most of them are imperatives. And there are four lengthy conditional constructions: if...then. I believe there are more imperatives and conditions per line in this passage than in any other passage in Mark.

It isn't just the fact of the imperatives that bothers me. After all, every theologian knows that there is an important place and time in the Christian life for the imperative. The thing that really bothers me is the content of these imperatives. "If your hand causes you to sin, cut if off." "If your foot causes you to sin, cut it off." "If your eye causes you to sin, pluck it out." If we took this passage at its face value, we would all be eating our meals with metal hooks strapped to the stubs of our arms, hobbling on crutches and groping our way from room to room.

The commentaries come to the rescue. They point out that the Jewish people never practiced self-mutilation of this kind. Some Gentile religions required their followers to cut off ears, fingers, genitals, but the Jewish people believed that God wanted them in their wholeness. So, this passage can only be hyperbole and is certainly not to be taken literally.

But behind every imperative is an indicative. And behind this text is Mark's belief that the rule of God (RSV: kingdom of God) is bursting into the world afresh. To appreciate what this meant for Mark, we need to remember that to him, the history of the world was divided into two parts: an old age ruled by Satan and a new age ruled by God.

If you want a picture of what the old age was like, just read the description of the Gerasene demoniac: "...who lived among the tombs and no one could bind him...even with a chain...the chains he wrenched apart and the fetters he broke in pieces; and no one had the strength to subdue him. Night and day among the tombs and on the mountains he was always crying out, and bruising himself with stones" (Mark 5:3–5, RSV). That, says Mark, is what existence is like apart from God.

But now, into the old age, comes Jesus whose very first words are: "The time is fulfilled, and the kingdom of God is at hand; repent, and believe in the gospel" (Mark 1:15, RSV). And sure enough, when Jesus encounters the Gerasene demoniac, the demoniac ends up "sitting there, clothed, and in his right mind" (Mark 5:15). For Mark, the exorcisms are demonstrations in miniature of what will happen when the rule of God comes bursting in its fullness into the cosmic order. Those who repent and believe in the gospel will be calmed and clothed for eternity, but those who do not are thrown into hell where the worm does not die and the fire is not quenched.

The indicative is the news that God is coming with something so wonderful, so attractive, so important that it would be worth an arm, or a leg, or an eye. Wouldn't you say that it is better to enter life maimed than to be thrown into hell with the worms roasting on the fire that never goes out?

Mark knows stories such as those told in 2 Maccabees. Seven Jewish brothers and their mother are arrested during the time when a Gentile king controlled the land of Israel. They were "compelled by the king, under torture with whips and cords, to partake of unlawful swine's flesh. One of them, acting as their spokesman, said, 'What do you intend to ask and learn from us? For we are ready to die rather than transgress the law of our fathers.' The king fell into a rage and gave orders that pans and caldrons be heated. These were heated immediately, and he commanded that the tongue of their spokesman be cut out and that they scalp him and *cut off his hands and feet*, while the rest of the brothers and the mother looked on. When he was utterly helpless, the king ordered them to take him to the fire, still breathing, and to fry him in a pan. The smoke from the pan spread widely, but the brothers and their mother encouraged one another to die nobly, saying, 'The Lord God is watching over us and in truth has compassion on us'" (2 Maccabees 7:1–6, RSV, emphasis mine).

Surely anyone in the world of Mark who heard our text would remember stories such as this—stories of Jewish people who saw something so valuable, so important, that they gave themselves for it rather than betray it. They did not mutilate themselves, but they gave themselves. It was worth an arm and a leg to remain faithful to the covenant with God.

Now, we no longer share Mark's apocalyptic worldview. We no longer think of demons in quite the way that Mark did and likely we do not think of God's rule coming into the world in quite the same way as Mark. Few of us will come face to face with tyrants with the same force as did the mother and her seven sons.

But, sometimes it seems that this world in which we live is trying as hard as it can to mutilate itself. Right now, for instance, you get the impression from some of the news reporters that the Olympic games are really a showdown between the good people and the bad people, and some of the media personalities are sad because the bad people are going back behind the iron curtain with more than their share of gold medals. Day by day we are hearing about unrest and violence in Burma, Haiti, Poland, South Africa, and a hundred other nations. And did you hear the story on the radio the other night about the children who just walk away? They aren't abducted. They suffer from something like what we would call ontological anxiety, and sometimes they just walk away and get lost.

The good news of the gospel is that though this world in which we live is bruising itself with stones, God loves it all. This is the heart of Mark's apocalyptic theology—that God loves the world so much that God wants to make it a fit place to live.

When we realize this, we come to understand ourselves as valuable not because of what we do but because we are loved by God. And we come to see our neighbors as valuable, not because of what they can do for us, but because God loves them and wills good for them. And when we realize this, a new world does begin to emerge, a world in which every person in every relationship is treated as a person who is loved endlessly by God. And when we see God's beautiful love and the new world coming from it, doesn't it cause us to rearrange all our priorities? Isn't it a thing of such beauty, such promise, such attraction, that we want to do whatever we can to say "Yes!"?

The dateline in the *New York Times* read, "Scottsbluff, Nebraska." "Right about 2 o'clock in the morning on those special

Saturdays when the automobile turns southeast onto State Highway 92, Harold and Polly Gentry and Darrell and Dee Willet, two retired couples, begin another autumn adventure. For miles and miles, theirs is almost always the only car on the two-lane highway through the middle of the night. They watch out for deer as they pass ranches and leave the darkened sandhills in the Nebraska panhandle.....An hour disappears as the car passes from Mountain to Central Time, and soon, about a half-hour before their 8:00 a.m. breakfast stop.....a large orange sun appears on the horizon to signal the start of a football Saturday." They get up at 2:00 a.m. They stay up all day and do not return home until 2:00 a.m. the next day. And why? To see a football game.

If people will give of themselves that much to watch a football game, how much should we give of ourselves on behalf of God's love and the new world it brings?

My wife went to Chicago for three weeks. Actually, she left one morning and was coming home the next night, but with me at home alone with the four children, it *seemed* like three weeks. On the night she was gone, dinner was like a scene out of a Star Wars cartoon show. But when we heard her hand on the door, we all came running. Our older son stopped bouncing on the jumping bed in the basement and came racing upstairs. Our older daughter put down the book to which she had been magnetized. Our younger daughter dropped her doll and our youngest child left his dish of ice cream on the dining room table. I got up from my desk and stumbled towards her with arms outstretched. We all came running because love had come into our house. She calms us and clothes us and put us in our right minds. And we'll do anything—yes, almost anything—to be with her.

Love has come into this world for you and me. Don't you want to say "Yes!" with everything you've got?

A Log in the Eye of the Text[5]

Text: "Judge not, that you be not judged. For with the judgment you pronounce you will be judged, and the measure you give will be the measure you get. Why do you see the speck that is in your brother's eye, but do not notice the log that is in your own eye? Or how can you say to your brother, 'Let me take the speck out of your eye,' when there is the log in your own eye? *You hypocrite*, first take the log out of your own eye, and then you will see clearly to take the speck out of your brother's eye."

Matthew 7:1–6, RSV

Orientation: The occasion for this sermon was very simple. It was my turn to preach in our seminary chapel schedule, and this text was the gospel reading in the lectionary for that week. As one who has worked for some time in the area of relations between Christians and Jews, I was quite aware of Matthew's proclivity to be somewhat heavy-handed in his treatment of Jews and Jewish authorities. Although this is not the place to discuss it, Matthew seems to have a more developed theology of displacement of Jews than does Mark; certainly he frequently adds displacement interpretations to materials that he borrows from Mark. But the real problem that occasioned the sermon, after I had re-read the text, was simply that the form of the text—with its blast against "you hypocrite" right in the middle of it—undercut the text's own message. The result is that the point Matthew wanted to make—how we should live in the light of the gospel—got undermined by the way Matthew went about making it. So I preached the sermon as I did to free up Matthew's message from the mold into which Matthew cast it. Part of the sermon undertakes the responsibility of setting the teachings of Jesus presented in the text in the context of the Palestinian Judaism of the time in order to help undercut the charge of hypocrisy made in the text and to locate Jesus in God's revelatory history with the people Israel.

The Sermon

Our text from the Gospel According to Matthew presents us with something of a paradox. On the one hand it is a fine piece of Christian teaching, reminding us that we should not be judgmental in our relationships with each other. It does not, by the way, command us not to exercise discretion or discernment, which would be foolish in the extreme, but to avoid being judgmental, which is quite another matter. The gospel tells us of the love of God for each and all, ourselves included, and commands us to love our neighbors as ourselves, to treat them as we would have them treat us.

On the other hand, the text itself contains a glaring example of the very sin against which it warns us. "You hypocrite," it declares, "first take the log out of your own eye." Here is definitely a case where the medium undermines the message. The message is: Do not be judgmental. The medium is: "You hypocrite!" It's as though we tried to teach our children not to engage in name-calling by saying: "Quit name-calling, *jerk*!" The text that warns us against the sin of being judgmental commits the very sin against which it preaches. What Matthew's Jesus says of the Pharisees in the invective of chapter 23 applies here to the way Matthew describes Jesus' teaching: It does not practice what it preaches. There is a log in the eye of the text.

Actually, the log seems to be in Matthew's eye (whoever Matthew was). Matthew liked to call people "hypocrites." Of the eighteen occurrences of the word "hypocrite(s)" in the New Testament, fourteen are in Matthew. If it weren't for Matthew, Christians might be less prone to think of other people as hypocrites. After all, most hypocrites are other people, aren't they? Seldom do we hear a person say, "I am a hypocrite." That's an entirely appropriate confession that we could all make. "You are a hypocrite," however, while doubtless true (who isn't a hypocrite, after all?), is a form of *tua culpa*, not *mea culpa*. We can say the latter only after we have said the former.

If we read Matthew's fourteen references to those whom he called "hypocrites" in context, we find out who Matthew thinks the hypocrites are. In Matthew 6:2 and 6:5, "the hypocrites" are found in *synagogues*! They are, you guessed it, *Jews*! The "hypocrites" of our text are still the ones addressed in chapter 6—all in the context of Matthew's long discourse called the Sermon on the Mount. In Matthew 15, Jesus calls the scribes and Pharisees "you hypocrites," and in chapter 22 it is the Pharisees, their disciples, and the Herodians who are hypocrites. In the diatribe that is chapter 23, "the scribes and Pharisees" are called "hypocrites" *five times*. Finally, in

24:51, we learn that the ultimate fate of the hypocrites will be distinctly unpleasant; when the "son of man" comes they will be put where they will weep and gnash their teeth. No doubt that'll teach them a lesson, by golly.

In Matthew, Jews are hypocrites and hypocrites are Jews. Gentiles come in for criticism in Matthew, but only Jews are hypocrites. Whether Matthew thought so or not, I am not competent to judge, but certainly the tradition of Christian anti-Jewish rhetoric came to see Jews and Judaism as essentially, necessarily, and by definition hypocritical. Christians have long charged Jews both with being self-righteous if they keep the law and hypocritical if they do not.

The other side of the paradox is that Matthew was right when he passed on the remark: "Judge not, that you be not judged. For with the judgment you pronounce, you will be judged." I suggest that it is appropriate to criticize Matthew's name-calling in the light of Matthew's own teaching against being judgmental. It is Matthew's own teaching that requires us to reject Matthew's own, frequent recourse to judgmentalism.

Because of the polemic against Jews and Judaism that came into the literature produced by the church in the last third of the first century, the period when the Gospels were put together, Jews and Judaism have ever since served the purposes of Christian polemic by standing for everything bad and negative in religion. It's as though the early church had a zero-sum understanding of the grace of God—that there wasn't enough of it to go around and therefore, if we got it the Jews couldn't, and vice versa. This trade-off mentality entered the church's teaching early.

The commandment not to be judgmental is one of the finest expressions of what it means to live the Christian life of love toward the neighbor. How can we learn to apply this commandment to the way we talk about Judaism and the Jewish people? How can we get the log out of our own eye, and out of our texts, when we look at or think about Jews and Judaism? How can we come to see clearly?

One rather simple way is by admitting that being judgmental is our problem before it is somebody else's, by learning to say, "I have sinned" before saying, "you have sinned." Yet another way is to recognize that the commandment to judge not is one that we have learned from Judaism. Let me explain.

Where did Matthew and/or Jesus before him get the idea that we should judge not, lest we be judged? Answer: Hillel, an older contemporary of Jesus and, along with Shammai, one of the two leading teachers in Judaism at the time, is cited in the Mishnah as having said: "Judge not thy fellowman until thou art come into his place." Hillel's teaching does not mean that we should refrain from being judgmental because we want to be nice to our moral inferiors. Hillel means that we should judge not because we don't know what we're talking about. You don't have it to judge on or to judge with. So quit judging. That's what Hillel and Jesus mean.

According to the Babylonian Talmud, Rabbi Abin said: "He who calls down divine judgment on his neighbor is himself punished first for his own sins." Because God is regularly characterized in the Hebrew Bible and Jewish tradition as a God of *chesed* (steadfast and long-suffering love), as a God who pardons iniquity and passes by transgression, the same tractate declares that those who have a right to retribution against another because of a crime committed, and yet waive it, will have all their own sins forgiven.

Our reading from Matthew talks about taking the log out of our own eyes first and then being able to see the speck in our neighbor's eye. This saying was a popular Palestinian folk saying about individuals who either refuse to accept criticism or who are quick to notice in others faults which they do not see in themselves. Rabbi Tarfon wondered whether anyone in his generation accepted criticism, "for if one say to him, 'Remove the mote from between your eyes,' he would answer, 'Remove the beam from between your eyes.'" In other popular forms the saying went: "Do not taunt your neighbor with the blemish which you have." And, "He who accuses another of fault, has it himself." Or: "Correct yourself and then correct others."

So it is to Jews, whom the text pillories as hypocrites, that we owe these wonderful sayings against being judgmental and engaging in name-calling. The gospel reminds us that we are to deal graciously with all our neighbors because God deals graciously with us. In all things, we are to use our best judgment, to be wise as serpents. But with all persons, we are to avoid being judgmental; we are to be innocent as doves. That is, we are to be hardheaded and softhearted, not softheaded and hard-hearted. Particularly, but by no means exclusively, with Jews and Judaism, to whom we owe these insights about how to live before God and with one another, we are to live in love and justice. Judge not that you be not judged. Indeed.

Notes

[1]Of course, any homiletical theory should satisfy these criteria. It should call upon the preacher to regard the listeners and the world as loved unconditionally by God and as the objects of God's will for justice. Its principles of communication should call for the sermon itself to be loving and just in the very way in which it is presented to the listeners. Any homiletical theory should be intelligible and account sensibly for the actual experience of the congregation and for the ways in which they receive and process communications. And, of course, it should not only advocate moral guidelines for the listeners' daily living but the manner of communication between preacher and congregation should itself be moral and never manipulative or abusive. The preacher is always under obligation to respect the freedom of the listeners.

[2]Of course, a good theory requires capable preachers. An insensitive, inchoate, unprepared minister can turn the best theory into bad preaching. And, the circumstances of the preaching event can interfere with the communication environment. For instance, a hot, humid day in an un-air-conditioned sanctuary is not the best climate for listener receptivity. A child eating lipstick from mother's purse may claim more of her attention than does the Word of God.

[3]For examples of other sermons which are developed in process perspective, see William A. Beardslee, *et al.*, *Biblical Preaching on the Death of Jesus*, pp. 130-135, 200-205; Charles W. Allen, "The Sign of Jonah," *Encounter*, Vol. 51 (1990), pp. 191-194; Charles R. Blaisdell, "The View from the Streets," in *The 1989 Ministers' Manual*, ed. James W. Cox (San Francisco: Harper & Row, 1988), p. 296f., *Encounter*, Vol. 49 (1988), contains a series of sermons informed by process thinking.

[4]A part of the sermon appeared in *The Christian Ministry*, Vol. 21, No. 1 (1990), p. 30f, and appears here by permission of the Christian Century Foundation.

[5]In an earlier form and with a different title, this sermon appeared in *Encounter*, Vol. 49, No. 1 (Winter 1988), pp. 63-65.

Bibliography

Achtemeier, Paul J. "*Omne verbum sonat*: The New Testament and the Oral Environment of Late Western Antiquity." *Journal of Biblical Literature*, Vol. 109, No. 1 (Spring 1990), pp. 3-27.

Allen, Charles W. "The Sign of Jonah." *Encounter*, Vol. 51, No. 2 (Spring 1990), pp. 191-194.

Allen, Ronald J. "The Social Function of Language in Preaching." In *Preaching as a Social Act*, ed. Arthur Van Seters. Nashville: Abingdon Press, 1988.

Anselm. *Basic Writings*, tr. S. N. Deane. LaSalle, IL: Open Court Publishing Co., 1962.

Anselm. "The Attributes of God." In *Readings in Christian Theology*, ed. Peter C. Hodgson and Robert H. King. Philadelphia: Fortress Press, 1985.

Aquinas, Thomas. "On the Production of Woman." In *Women and Religion*, ed. Elizabeth Clark and Herbert Richardson. New York: Harper & Row, 1977, pp. 85-101.

Augustine. *On Christian Doctrine*, tr. D. W. Robertson, Jr. Indianapolis: Bobbs-Merrill, 1958.

Augustine. *On the Psalms 134:3–6.* In *Documents in Early Christian Thought*, ed. Maurice Wiles and Mark Santer. Cambridge: Cambridge University Press, 1975, pp. 17-21.

Augustine. "On Marriage and Concupiscence." In *Women and Religion*, ed. Elizabeth Clark and Herbert Richardson. New York: Harper & Row, 1977, pp. 72-77.

Bailey, Lloyd. "The Lectionary in Critical Perspective." *Interpretation*, Vol. 31 (1977), pp. 139-153.

Baptism, Eucharist, Ministry. Geneva: World Council of Churches, 1982.

Baron, Harold M. "The Web of Urban Racism." In *Institutional Racism in America*, ed. Louis L. Knowles and Kenneth Prewitt. Englewood Cliffs, NJ: Prentice-Hall, Inc., 1969, pp.134-176.

Barr, James. *The Scope and Authority of the Bible.* Philadelphia: Westminster Press, 1980.

Barth, Karl. *The Humanity of God*, tr. J. N. Thomas and T. Weiser. Richmond: John Knox Press, 1960.

Beardslee, William A., Cobb, John B., Jr., Lull, David J., Pregeant, Russell, Weeden, Theodore J., Sr., and Woodbridge, Barry A. *Biblical Preaching on the Death of Jesus.* Nashville: Abingdon Press, 1989.

Beardslee, William A. *A House for Hope.* Philadelphia: Westminster Press, 1972.

Beardslee, William A. "Openness to the New in Apocalyptic and in Process Theology." *Process Studies*, Vol. 3 (1973), pp. 169-178.

Beardslee, William A. "Recent Hermeneutics and Process Thought." *Process Studies*, Vol. 12, No. 2 (1982), pp. 65-76.

Berger, Peter and Luckmann, Thomas. *The Social Construction of Reality.* New York: Doubleday, 1966.

Birch, Charles and Cobb, John B., Jr. *The Liberation of Life: From the Cell to the Community.* Cambridge: Cambridge University Press, 1981.

Blaisdell, Charles. "Speak to the Heart of Jerusalem: The 'Conversational' Structure of Deutero-Isaiah." *Encounter*, Vol. 52, No. 1 (Winter 1991), forthcoming.

Blaisdell, Charles. "The View from the Streets." In *The 1989 Ministers' Manual*, ed. James W. Cox. San Francisco: Harper & Row, 1988, pp. 296-297.

Bolingen, Dwight. *Language: The Loaded Weapon.* New York: Longmans, 1980.

Bonhoeffer, Dietrich. *The Cost of Discipleship*, tr. H. R. Fuller. New York: Macmillan, 1963.

Boulding, Kenneth. *The Image*. Ann Arbor: University of Michigan, 1956.

Bower, Peter. *Handbook for the Common Lectionary*. Philadelphia: Geneva, 1987.

Brock, Rita Nakashima. *Journeys by Heart*. New York: Crossroad, 1988.

Brown, Delwin. "'Respect for the Rocks:' Toward a Christian Process Theology of Nature." *Encounter*, Vol. 50 (Autumn 1989), pp. 309-321.

Brown, Delwin. *To Set at Liberty*. Maryknoll: Orbis Books, 1981.

Brown, Frank Burch. *Transfiguration: Poetic Metaphor and the Languages of Religious Belief*. Chapel Hill: University of North Carolina Press, 1983.

Brown, Frank Burch. "Transfiguration: Poetic Metaphor and Theological Reflection," *The Journal of Religion*, Vol. 62 (January 1982), pp. 39-56.

Brueggemann, Walter. *Genesis*, Interpretation Commentary. Atlanta: John Knox Press, 1982.

Buechner, Frederick. *Wishful Thinking*. New York: Harper & Row, 1973.

Burrell, David B. "The Spirit and the Christian Life." In *Christian Theology: Its Traditions and Tasks*, ed. Peter C. Hodgson and Robert H. King. Philadelphia: Fortress Press, 1985, pp. 302-327.

Buttrick, David G. *Homiletic*. Philadelphia: Fortress Press, 1987.

Buttrick, David G. "Interpretation and Preaching," *Interpretation*, Vol. 25 (1981), pp. 59-71.

Calvin, John. *Institutes of the Christian Religion*, ed. John T. McNeill, tr. Ford L. Battles. Philadelphia: Westminster Press, 1950.

Calvin, John. "God's Providence Governs All." In *Readings in Christian Theology*, ed. Peter C. Hodgson and Robert H. King. Philadelphia: Fortress Press, 1985, pp. 123-128.

Campbell, Alexander. *The Christian System* (Reprint Edition). Salem, NH: Ayer Co., 1988.

Carr, Anne E. *Transforming Grace*. San Francisco: Harper & Row, 1988.

Chopp, Rebecca S. *The Power to Speak*. New York: Crossroad, 1989.

Chopp, Rebecca S. *The Praxis of Suffering*. Maryknoll: Orbis Books, 1986.

Clement of Alexandria. *Miscellanies*, Vol. 5, No. xii, pp. 78-82. In *Documents In Early Christian Thought*, ed. Maurice Wiles and Mark Santer. Cambridge: Cambridge University Press, 1975, pp. 4-7.

Cobb, John B., Jr., and Birch, Charles. *The Liberation of Life*. Cambridge: Cambridge University Press, 1981.

Cobb, John B., Jr., *Praying for Jennifer*. Nashville: The Upper Room, 1985.

Cobb, John B., Jr., "The Presence of the Past and the Eucharist." *Process Studies*, Vol. 13 (1983), pp. 218-231.

Cobb, John B., Jr., *Process Theology as Political Theology*. Philadelphia: Westminster Press, 1982.

Cobb, John B., Jr., *Talking About God* (with David Tracy). New York: The Seabury Press, 1983.

Cobb, John B., Jr., and Griffin, David R. *Process Theology*. Philadelphia: Westminster, 1976.

The Common Lectionary. New York: The Church Hymnal Corporation, 1983.

Cross, Theodore. *The Black Power Imperative*. New York: Faulkner Books, 1987.

Dombrowski, Daniel A. *Hartshorne and the Metaphysics of Animal Rights*. Albany: State University of New York Press, 1988.

Dunn, James D. G. *Jesus, Paul and the Law*. Louisville: Westminster/ John Knox Press, 1990.

Ehrlich, Paul R., *et al.. The Cold and the Dark*. New York: Norton, 1984.

Fact Sheets on Institutional Racism. Compiled by the Council on Interracial Books for Children, Inc., New York: 1984.

Farley, Edward. *Theologia*. Philadelphia: Fortress Press, 1983.

Faulkner, Joseph E. "What Are They Saying?" In *A Case Study of Mainstream Protestantism*, ed. D. Newell Williams (Grand Rapids: Eerdmans, and St. Louis: Chalice Press, 1991).

Felix, Minucius. *Octavius*. In *The Ante-Nicene Fathers*, Vol. IV, ed. A. Roberts and J. Donaldson. Grand Rapids: Eerdmans, 1979, pp. 173-198.

Ford, Lewis. *The Lure of God*. Philadelphia, Fortress Press, 1978. Franklin, Stephen T. *Speaking from the Depths*. Grand Rapids, William B. Eerdmans, 1990.

Gadamer, Hans-Georg. *Truth and Method*, tr. G. Barding and J. Cumming. New York: Crossroad, 1975.

Gaston, Lloyd. *Paul and the Torah*. Vancouver: University of British Columbia Press, 1987.

Gilkey, Langdon. "God." In *Christian Theology: An Introduction to Its Traditions and Tasks*, ed. Peter C. Hodgson and Robert H. King. Philadelphia: Fortress Press, 1985, pp. 88-113.

Gilkey, Langdon. *Naming the Whirlwind*. Indianapolis: Bobbs-Merrill, 1969.

Gilkey, Langdon. "Plurality and Its Theological Implications." In *The Myth of Christian Uniqueness*, ed. John Hick and Paul F. Knitter. Maryknoll: Orbis Books, 1987, pp. 37-50.

Gonzales, Justo and Catherine. *Liberation Preaching*. Nashville: Abingdon Press, 1980.

Gregory, Dick. *Dick Gregory's Bible Tales*. New York: Harper & Row, 1974.

Griffin, David Ray (ed.) *The Reenchantment of Science*. Albany: State University of New York Press, 1988.

Guth, James L., and Turner, Helen Lee. "Pastoral Politics in the 1988 Election: Disciples as Compared to Presbyterians and Southern Baptists." In *A Case Study of Mainstream Protestantism*, ed. D. Newell Williams (Grand Rapids: Eerdmans, and St. Louis: Chalice Press, 1991).

148   *A Credible and Timely Word*

1111111

148   *A Credible and Timely Word*

Kelsey, David H. "The Theological Use of Scripture in Process Hermeneutics." *Process Studies*, Vol. 13, No. 3 (1983), pp. 181-188.

Klotz, John W. *Ecology Crisis*. St. Louis: Concordia, 1971.

Knowles, Louis L., and Prewitt, Kenneth, eds. *Institutional Racism in America*. Englewood Cliffs, NJ: Prentice-Hall, Inc., 1969.

Kraus, Hans-Joachim. *Psalms 60-150*, tr. Hilton C. Oswald. Minneapolis: Augsburg, 1989.

Lakhoff, George and Johnson, Mark. *Metaphors We Live By*. Chicago: University of Chicago Press, 1980.

Lamb, Matthew L. "Liberation Theology and Social Justice." *Process Studies*, Vol. 14 (1985), pp. 102-123.

Langer, Susanne K. *Feeling and Form*. New York: Charles Scribner's Sons, 1953.

Langer, Susanne K. *Philosophical Sketches*. Baltimore: Johns Hopkins, 1962.

Langer, Susanne K. *Philosophy in a New Key*. Cambridge: Harvard University Press, 1942.

Langer, Susanne K. *Problems in Art*. New York: Charles Scribner's Sons, 1957.

Lee, Bernard J. *The Galilean Jewishness of Jesus*. New York: Paulist Press, 1988.

Long, Thomas G. "The Fall of the House of Uzzah and Other Difficult Preaching Texts." *Journal for Preachers*, Vol. 7 (1983), pp. 13-19.

Long, Thomas G. *Preaching and the Literary Forms of the Bible*. Philadelphia: Fortress, 1989.

Lull, David J. *The Spirit in Galatia*, SBL Dissertation Series. Chico: Scholars Press, 1980.

Lull, David J. "What Is 'Process Hermeneutics'?" *Process Studies*, Vol. 13, No. 3 (1983), pp. 189-201.

Luther, Martin. *Commentary on St. Paul's Epistle to the Galatians*. In *Martin Luther: Selections*, ed. John Dillenberger. Garden City: Anchor Books, 1961, pp. 99-165.

Manchester Guardian Weekly. August 14, 1988, Vol. 139, No. 7. Manchester, England: Guardian Publications Ltd.

Mason, David R. "Reflections on Prayer from a Process Perspective." *Encounter*, Vol. 45, No. 5 (Autumn 1989), pp. 347-359.

McDaniel, Jay B. *Of God and Pelicans.* Louisville: Westminster/John Knox Press, 1989.

McFague, Sallie. *Metaphorical Theology.* Philadelphia: Fortress Press, 1982.

McFague, Sallie. *Models of God.* Philadelphia: Fortress Press, 1987.

Meland, Bernard E. *Fallible Forms and Symbols.* Philadelphia: Fortress Press, 1976.

Mills, C. Wright. *The Causes of World War Three.* New York: Simon and Schuster, 1958.

Myrdal, Gunnar. *An American Dilemma.* New York: Harper & Row, 1964.

Niebuhr, H. Richard. *The Meaning of Revelation.* New York: Macmillan, 1941.

Niebuhr, H. Richard. *Radical Monotheism and Western Culture.* New York: Harper & Row, 1960.

Niebuhr, Reinhold. *Moral Man and Immoral Society.* New York: Charles Scribner's Sons, 1932.

Niebuhr, Reinhold. *The Nature and Destiny of Man*, Vol. II. New York: Charles Scribner's Sons, 1953.

Ogden, Schubert M. "Ask and It Will Be Given You." In *Rockefeller Chapel Sermons*, comp. Donovan E. Smucker. Chicago: The University of Chicago Press, 1966, pp. 98-109.

Ogden, Schubert M. "The Metaphysics of Faith and Justice." *Process Studies*, Vol. 14 (1985), pp. 87-101.

Ogden, Schubert M. *On Theology.* New York: Harper & Row, 1986.

Ogden, Schubert M. *The Point of Christology.* New York: Harper & Row, 1982.

Ogden, Schubert M. *The Reality of God*. New York: Harper & Row, 1966.

Ogden, Schubert M. "The Service of Theology to the Servant Task of Pastoral Ministry." In *The Pastor as Servant*, ed. E. Earl Shelp and Ronald D. Sunderland. New York: Pilgrim Press,1986.

Ogden, Schubert M. "Toward a New Theism." In *Process Philosophy and Christian Thought*, ed. Delwin Brown, Ralph E. James, Jr., and Gene Reeves. Indianapolis: Bobbs-Merrill, 1971, pp. 173-187.

Origen. *Homilies on Jeremiah 18:7-10*. In *Documents in Early Christian Thought*, ed. M. Wiles and M. Santer. Cambridge: Cambridge University Press, 1975: pp. 7-10.

Osborn, Ronald E., ed. *Seeking God's Peace in a Nuclear Age*. St. Louis: CBP Press, 1985.

Pagels, Elaine. *Adam, Eve and the Spirit*. New York: Random House, 1988.

Perrin, Norman. *Rediscovering the Teaching of Jesus*. New York: Harper & Row, 1976.

Perrin, Norman and Duling, Dennis. *The New Testament: An Interpretation*. New York: Harcourt, Brace, Jovanovich, 1982.

Pittenger, Norman. *Freed to Love*. New York: Morehouse Barlow, 1987.

Pittenger, Norman. *Life as Eucharist*. Grand Rapids: Eerdmans, 1973.

Pittenger, Norman. *Praying Today*. Grand Rapids: William B. Eerdmans, 1974.

Pregeant, Russell. *Christology Beyond Dogma*, SBL Semeia Supplements. Missoula: Scholars Press, 1978.

Pregeant, Russell. *Mystery Without Magic*. Oak Park: Meyer- Stone Books, 1988.

Ricoeur, Paul *Freud and Philosophy*, tr. Denis Savage. New Haven: Yale University Press, 1970.

Ricoeur, Paul. *Interpretation Theory*. Fort Worth: Texas Christian University Press, 1976.

Ricoeur, Paul. "Naming God." *Union Seminary Quarterly Review*, Vol. 34 (1979), pp. 215-227.

Rieser, M. "Brief Introduction to the Epistemology of Art." *Journal of Philosophy*, Vol. 47 (1950), pp. 695-704.

Ritschl, Albrecht. *The Christian Doctrine of Justification and Reconciliation*, tr. H. R. Mackintosh. New York: Charles Scribner's Sons, 1900.

Roberts, D. Bruce. "Theological Education and Field Education: A Parallel Process." Lecture, Christian Theological Seminary.

Russell, John M. "Pittenger on Prayer: A Process Apologia." *Encounter*, Vol. 50, No. 4 (Autumn 1989), pp. 337-351.

Russell, Letty. *Human Liberation in a Feminist Perspective—A Theology*. Philadelphia: Westminster Press, 1974.

Sanders, E. P. *Paul, the Law, and the Jewish People*. Philadelphia: Fortress Press, 1983.

Sanders, James A. "Canon and Calendar: An Alternative Lectionary Proposal." In Dieter T. Hessell, ed., *Social Themes of the Christian Year*. Philadelphia: Geneva, 1983.

Sanders, James A. *Canon and Community*. Philadelphia: Fortress Press, 1984.

Skudlarek, William. *The Word in Worship*. Nashville: Abingdon, 1981.

Stark, Rodney, *et al.*, *Wayward Shepherds*. New York: Harper & Row, 1971.

Sturm, Douglas. *Community and Alienation: Essays on Process Thought and Public Life*. Notre Dame: University of Notre Dame Press, 1988.

Suchocki, Marjorie Hewitt. *God, Christ, Church*. New York: Crossroad, 1982.

Tennis, Diane. *Is God the Only Reliable Father?* Philadelphia: Westminster Press, 1985.

Toplady, Augustus. "Rock of Ages." *The Hymnal*. Philadelphia: Presbyterian Board of Christian Education, 1938, p. 237.

Tracy, David. *The Analogical Imagination*. New York: Crossroad, 1981.

Tracy, David. *Blessed Rage for Order*. New York: Seabury Press, 1978.

Tracy, David. *Plurality and Ambiguity*. San Francisco: Harper & Row, 1987.

Tracy, David. *A Short History of the Interpretation of the Bible* (with Robert M. Grant). Philadelphia: Fortress Press, 1984.

Trible, Phyllis. *God and the Rhetoric of Sexuality*. Philadelphia: Fortress Press, 1978.

Wainwright, Geoffrey. *Doxology*. New York: Oxford University Press, 1980.

Watkins, Keith. *Faithful and Fair*. Nashville: Abingdon Press, 1981.

Watkins, Keith. *Liturgies in a Time When Cities Burn*. Nashville: Abingdon Press, 1969.

Watkins, Keith, ed. *Thankful Praise*. St. Louis: CBP Press, 1987.

Weeden, Theodore J. "The Potential and Promise of a Process Hermeneutic." *Encounter*, Vol. 36, No. 4 (Autumn 1975), pp. 316-330.

White, James F. *Introduction to Christian Worship*. Nashville: Abingdon Press, 1980.

White, Lynn. "The Historical Roots of Our Ecological Crisis." *Science*, Vol. 155 (1967), pp. 1203-1207.

Whitehead, Alfred North. *Modes of Thought*. New York: Macmillan, 1938.

Whitehead, Alfred North. *Religion in the Making*. New York: Meridian Books, 1960.

Whitehead, Alfred North. *Science and the Modern World*. New York: The New American Library, 1925.

Whitehead, Alfred North. *Process and Reality*, Corrected Edition. New York: The Free Press, 1978.

Whitehead, Alfred North. *Adventures of Ideas*. New York: Macmillan, 1933.

Wieman, Henry Nelson. *The Source of Human Good*. Carbondale: Southern Illinois University Press, 1946.

Williamson, Clark M. "The Authority of Scripture After the *Shoah*," in *Faith and Creativity*, ed. George Nordgulen and George W. Shields (St. Louis: CBP Press, 1987), pp. 125-142.

Williamson, Clark M. *God Is Never Absent.* St. Louis: The Bethany Press, 1977.

Williamson, Clark M. "Good Stewards of God's Varied Grace," *Encounter*, Vol. 47, No. 1 (Winter 1986), pp. 61-83.

Williamson, Clark M. *Has God Rejected His People?* Nashville: Abingdon Press, 1982.

Williamson, Clark M. and Allen, Ronald J. *Interpreting Difficult Texts.* London: SCM and Philadelphia: Trinity Press, 1989.

Williamson, Clark M. "The Lord's Supper: A Systematic Theo- logical View." *Encounter*, Vol. 50, No. 1 (Winter 1989), pp. 47-67.

Williamson, Clark M. "Process Hermeneutics and Christianity's Post-Holocaust Reinterpretation of Itself." *Process Studies*, Vol. 12, No. 2 (Summer 1982), pp. 77-93.

Williamson, Clark M. and Allen Ronald J. *The Teaching Minister.* Louisville: Westminster/John Knox Press, 1991.

Wink, Walter. *Naming the Powers.* Philadelphia: Fortress Press, 1984.

Wink, Walter. *Unmasking the Powers.* Philadelphia: Fortress Press, 1986.

Wire, Antoinette C. "The Structure of the Gospel Miracle Stories and Their Tellers." *Semeia*, Vol. 11 (1978), pp. 83-114.

Woodbridge, Barry A. "An Assessment and Prospectus for a Process Hermeneutics." *Journal of the American Academy of Religion*, Vol. XLVII, No. 1 (March 1979), pp. 121-128.

Wren, Brian. *What Language Shall I Borrow?* New York: Crossroad, 1989.

Young, Henry James. *Hope in Process: A Theology of Social Pluralism.* Philadelphia: Fortress Press, 1990.